Mint Chocolate Chip

Choices to Live By

Alan E. Sargent

VMI PUBLISHERS • SISTERS, OREGON

Published by
TrustedBooks
VMI Publishers
Sisters, Oregon
www.vmipublishers.com

ISBN: 1933204583
ISBN 13: 9781933204581
Library of Congress Control Number: 2008923110

Printed in the USA.
Cover design by Linda Braine

Mint Chocolate Chip

Introduction

Anyone who knows me knows that I love mint chocolate chip ice cream. Of course, I love ice cream of any flavor but given thirty-one to choose from or Ben and Jerry's menu, I'll still always pick mint chocolate chip. Some might say, "How boring!" And I suppose making the same choice every time might seem that way. But what if your choice is the best one? Do you choose differently next time for the sake of variety?! Sometimes the road not taken needs to remain so.

A student of mine once remarked, "Why is it that I always find what I'm looking for in the last place I look?" In a flash of revelation, I responded, "Because once you've found it you would be a fool to keep looking, wouldn't you?" In the same way our choices in life determine our outcomes. Whether we are suffering as the result of some unintended consequences of our own making or have become the collateral damage of someone else's boneheadedness (is that a word?), we have only to look back to see why: "Augh! I could have had a V8!"

Some may criticize the act of looking back, but since they have paid the costly price of experience, should they not make good use of the 20/20 hindsight it affords? The bard may sing of no regrets, but does he have amnesia, is he deluded, or is he just ignorant?

Regret gets a bad rap. I thank God for my regrets, and I have plenty of them. They are what make me choose the right path next time. **Regret is where the past meets the present to guide the future.**

What follows is a book of proverbs—wisdom I have gleaned from the choices I have made. Although written specifically to my own children, the truths conveyed are universal. Each proverb is followed by a parable or a poem. There are fifty-two entries so this book could serve as a weekly devotional, and I have written a prayer at the end of each one appropriate to the topic.

I have also chosen to include the personal letters I wrote to my children when I gave them their copy of this book. Perhaps it will give you some insight into my motivations.

Perhaps you are reading this introduction to decide if this book is worth your investment. If so, let me encourage you to empty your wallet! Don't just get one for yourself; buy one for every teenager on your block or every member of your church. If you could spare yourself or someone you love from just one bump in the road of life, wouldn't it be worth it? This is your opportunity to "choose wisely" ...**Mint Chocolate Chip**...is there really any other flavor out there?

Foreword

This book was begun with three individuals in mind: Jeremy, Jonathan, and Anna Sargent. Jeremy, my eldest, will turn thirty this year; Jonathan and Anna are twenty-eight and twenty-one respectively. When Jonathan married Michelle this past July, I broadened my audience with great joy. Should Jeremy and Anna marry and my children give me grandchildren, I will gladly increase my readership accordingly.

Today, as I send my manuscript off to the publisher, I will be increasing again the number in whose hands this work may fall. In my introduction, I even address those "others" who might be inspired to follow in my footsteps with their own literary contributions to still other recipients. In all of this, I do not want my own children to ever think my words were intended for anyone but them personally. What follows is the personal letter I wrote to them some twenty years ago. All other readers will, I trust, bear with me.

Acknowledgements

Any attempt to adequately list or appropriately thank those persons involved in helping me produce this work would fall short, I am sure. Nevertheless, I would not have been successful in this endeavor without the inspiration and support of my wonderful wife, Lynn, who is the subject of so much of what I have tried to impart to my children.

My earthly father, Ray L. Sargent, though deceased, has been and, as I reflect upon the input I have received from him, continues to be a source for much of the life lessons I have recorded here.

My thanks to Ralph Irwin, my longtime friend and an "uncle" to my children, for lovingly producing the illustrations included herein.

Thanks also to all of those people who have had their formative input into my life: Don and Hettie Lue Brooks, Beth Sargent and Maribeth Israel—godly grandmothers and mentors by example, and the pastors and teachers under whose input I have sat—Morris Cerullo, Bob Yandian, Terry Law, Jim Gilbert and Tim Brooks.

My Heavenly Father, of course, deserves the place of highest honor in this effort as His inspiration and the example of His Son, Jesus, were indispensable support. And I must thank the Holy Spirit for His role in the ongoing efforts to strengthen and encourage me to live out the high ideals I have set for myself and recommend to my children.

Table of Contents

Mint Chocolate Chip has been arranged in fifty-two entries and is intended to serve as a weekly devotional, but all the entry titles are listed below so they may be located by name and page number.

March 11, 1986

Dear Jeremy, Jonathan, and Anna:

While I was laying in my hospital bed in Knoxville, Tennessee, I began thinking about all those things I nearly never got the opportunity to do. One of the things that weighed heavily upon me was the thought that had I died in the accident, I never would have had the chance to help in your upbringing. I never would have been there for you when you came home from your first date; never would have been able to counsel you about the kind of friendships you should be fostering, or how to deal with the many victories and defeats of life.

For these reasons, I have decided to record here for you the wisdom that experience has taught me through the years. Some of these proverbs have been stated more eloquently by others, some are what I have gleaned in watching others, but all of them are original to me in their slant and wording.

Do your best to read between the lines for those shades of meaning that are particularly appropriate to your present circumstances. In no case let these words of advice and counsel conflict with your understanding of the Scriptures. I have tried in every case to keep my instruction within the contexts of the wisdom and accuracy of the Word of God.

Where appropriate, like Solomon, I have addressed you as "My Son" or "My Daughter." Consider this and the labor of such an undertaking as this as an indication of the measure of my love for you and of my desire for your success in every endeavor.

If I have learned anything in life at all, it is that there is no guarantee of tomorrow. I know that I will be able to rest easier with this project complete...secure in the knowledge that I have made an important step forward in the task of fulfilling the responsibilities of Fatherhood.

Never take your responsibility as a father or a mother lightly. And when in the course of time you, too, begin to feel the weight of this responsibility, then make your own additions to this heritage I now give you.

P.S. November 17, 2006— It has been nearly 20 years since I began this project and now it is finally drawing to a close ... at least for this first volume. All of you, I trust, will be having children of your own in the near (or very near ... no pressure) future. May your own wisdom exceed mine.

ONE

Taker

Unrighteous passion is a sleeping monster which,
if awakened, will arise and violently destroy all that you hold dear.

He wept, a delicate rose now crushed,
Clutching too tightly the slender frond,
He'd held it close and homeward rushed,
Only to find its beauty gone.

His heart was broken o'er that bloom
Till seeing the face it paled beside;
Desire rekindled chased the gloom
No place for regrets reside.

Slowly wanting was left behind
'Twas lust and passion he proffered
Pressing beyond a reluctant mind
He took what was not offered.

His selfish ardor fully spent
His wicked hunger sated
He watched as off her beauty went
Another rose now faded.

Heavenly Father, be a watchman over the thoughts and intents of my children. Let your Holy Spirit so move as to help them quickly identify temptation to the end that sin be not conceived and unrighteousness be not given birth. Amen.

FOR ADDITIONAL READING: JAMES 1:14-15

Two

Playing Angel

Since the "borrower is servant to the lender" (a) and he that gives to the poor "lendeth unto the Lord," (b) then give and watch how the Lord becomes your servant in the meeting of your every need.

One of the most enjoyable blessings of my life has been the occasional opportunity to play "angel of mercy" to those I have seen in need. What makes this most pleasurable is anonymity.

I will never forget overhearing a conversation that a young couple was having about the empty condition of their cupboards. They were friends of mine and were both working hard as Y-Camp directors for much less money than they could have made elsewhere. I felt the Lord clearly speak to me to help them, so I bought them five sacks of groceries. I drove over to their neighborhood and parked close enough to be able to watch their coming and going and far enough away to not be detected. As a "starving" college student, I had been a frequent guest, and they had told me where they hid their house key. So, when they left in their station wagon, I deposited the groceries on their kitchen table. Before I could finish, I heard them pulling back into their garage, perhaps to retrieve something they had forgotten. I knew I couldn't go out the front unnoticed, so I quickly crept out the back door. I had just closed it when I heard the first squeal of delight from one of the kids.

"Daddy, look" she exclaimed! "An angel has been here." Her parents were not so easily convinced and went straight to the front door to look outside. I knew they would soon be opening the back door where I was crouched on the porch listening to them, so I took off like a shot out of a cannon and cleared the neighbor's six-foot privacy fence with the effortlessness of a gazelle. The adrenaline I had sufficed for an additional three fences, and I finally circled around to my car and drove off. What a rush!

Jehovah Jireh, I entreat you to bless my children with giving hearts; a heart of compassion and wisdom but not ignorant of the greater work of the heart you may be accomplishing through the circumstances of life. Amen.

For additional reading: Proverbs 11:24-25; Matthew 6:1-4; (a) Proverbs 22:7, (b) Proverbs 19:17

THREE

Leaning in Love

*My Son, you become old enough to begin the courtship process
when you reach the level of maturity that ensures
that you can do the following:
— Treat your young woman like a lady.
— Protect her from physical and emotional harm.
— Provide her an enjoyable experience, companionship, and
spiritual enrichment.*

Your mother is one of the few young ladies I didn't kiss on the first date. Somehow, it just didn't occur to me. I met her on Saturday morning the 12th of January, 1973. I was supposed to go out of town to minister to a youth group, but the weather had turned bitterly cold and an inch-thick sheet of glare ice covered the Tulsa streets. The minute I walked into the ORU Student Union Building (the "SUB" we called it), I caught a glimpse of Lynn. She was sitting next to a student from my Hebrew class which, of course, gave me the excuse I sought for an introduction. I shall never forget how cute she looked in her candy-striper hospital volunteer uniform. It was hard not just to gawk at her while Jeannie was introducing me…there was something in her eyes that captivated me.

(This was not the first time I had actually seen her. After returning from Christmas break she had been asked to share a testimony in chapel. On the plane home to Massachusetts, she apparently had sat next to the coach of the visiting basketball team that had just played ORU. She had an opportunity to witness to him and prayed with him for salvation. The Coach had called the school to share how much he appreciated this student, and the word had gotten back to Brother Bob, ORU's chaplain. As I sat listening to her share, I remember thinking how impressed I was with this girl.)

Later, that same evening, I attended a drama production performed by the Jeremiah People. Lynn was there, too, and I walked up to her after the performance. I commented that she looked like she hadn't eaten in days (not a remark I would recommend that you make to a girl you are trying to impress). I talked her into going to dinner with me so I could counsel with her about her emotional state (I am not making this up). You may think that this sounds like a pretty lame ploy, but it was all I could think up at the time. Seriously, my heart did go out to her as she shared with me about the relationship she had just ended. I took her to Steak and Ale and we talked way into the evening. After taking her back to the dorms, I prayed with her, escorted her up the steps and said good night.

We probably went out fifteen times before it occurred to me that I was romantically attracted to Lynn. Not because she wasn't pretty; quite the contrary. It's just that I didn't *fall* in love...I *leaned* in love first. When I did fall in love, we had already built a very secure friendship. I will never forget our first kiss. We were headed out of the parking lot to go somewhere and I looked over at her with new eyes. I said, "You don't *have* to hug the door handle." She slid over and the rest is, shall we say, history.

Lord, grant my sons the ability to see a young lady as her loving father's most valuable treasure and her big brother's most cherished prize. Amen.

FOR ADDITIONAL READING: EPHESIANS 5:1, 2, 25

Now, something personal from your mother's "private" collection.

To Lynn

(On the occasion of Valentine's Day, 1999)

It's hard to say when love began,
So delicate was its fashion,
I'd hardly noticed friendship's warmth
Become fire's burning passion.

The more time spent, just fanned the flame
Yet absence blew the harder,
For when apart near every thought
Of you pulsed with more ardor.

At first it seemed I leaned in love
But soon, myself full falling,
Prayed earnestly I'd read aright,
'Twas me those eyes were calling.

Twenty-six years since we first met,
One less now since our union;
Each day with you a sweet caress,
Each moment, rich communion.

Eternity's joys are beyond compare,
God's presence is unequaled,
But life with you has been so blessed,
'Twould suffice were it unsequeled.

By your loving husband

Alan Sargent

Four

Fence Post Miracle

*Imagination, curiosity, the joy of discovery, and
the pleasure of reading are the serious student's greatest assets.*

Whatever it takes to get your children to first, learn to read and then *love* to read, do it! Nothing quite stirs the soul or stimulates the imagination as does reading. The Native Americans were fascinated with the White Man's "talking leaves." The most noble tribe of the Cherokees was set apart by the brilliant efforts of one of their chiefs, Sequoyah, who alone of the tribes of North America created an alphabet and a written language for his people.

When I was in elementary school, the bookmobile would come by the school grounds for half a day on Thursdays during the summers. I remember the excitement and anticipation of turning in last week's stack for the new adventures that lay ahead. I had gained a love for reading by virtue of the escape it provided…not that my life was so horrible that I sought relief, but what of my mundane existence compared to the adventures of mountain-man Jim Bridger, or of explorers Lewis and Clark, or Zebulon Pike? I loved the biography section more than any other. A close second was science fiction. I read Heinlein's *Have Space Suit Will Travel* and Asimov's *Foundation* series and traveled to distant worlds my friends could never imagine. I also sailed with Horatio Hornblower, rode with the Rough Riders and "I Was There at the Oklahoma Land Run."

As I consider the influence reading has had on my life, I realize that from it I have gained a desire to make my life count like those of the awe-inspiring men who had accomplished such great deeds. Although you may be similarly inspired by a great song or a movie about men of heroic proportions, nothing seals those mental pictures in your mind so deeply as the process of creating a three-dimensional image from two-dimensional ink on paper.

When Jonathan was nine or ten, your Mom and I were concerned that all he enjoyed reading was "Garfield" comics. Valuing reading as we both do, we struck upon a plan. I knew that Jon wanted his own horse, but I had been resistant to his pleas due to the cost of fencing. That is when it occurred to me to offer a "reading incentive." For every ten pages of the books he read, of my choosing, I would buy one fence post. The first three fence posts came laboriously, but suddenly I found myself in a fence post financial crisis!

Jonathan became a voracious reader and has now begun a rewrite on his first 700+ page novel! Indeed "the pen is mightier than the sword."[1] More of this world has been changed by the force of written ideas than will ever be by force of might. *And, the key to the wielding of the pen is the turning of the page.* If you desire to have an influence on this earth of any lasting proportion, you must learn to write skillfully; and the more good reading you do, the more good writing you will produce.

Holy Spirit, as the Word promises, lead and guide my children into all truth. May the same Creative Mind that fashioned this world direct their drive to learn and their quest for excellence. Amen.

FOR ADDITIONAL READING: 2 TIMOTHY 2:15; DEUTERONOMY 17:18-20; JOHN 16:12, 13

FIVE

Hating Hypocrisy

Physical well-being: . . . . *You are what you eat.*
Mental well-being: . . . . *You are what you read.*
Spiritual well-being: . . . . *You are what you pray.*

I find it a constant source of amazement, when I look back upon the various influences of my life, to see how what I am today is their consequent product. This is not to say that I am merely the result of a sequence of coincidences, but rather the Director of this drama has been using each scene of each act to prepare me for the next, building my "character" as the play progresses.

An example of this is my aversion to hypocrisy. One experience stands out in my mind as the source of this disdain. Our family was over at the home of our parish priest sharing an evening of fellowship. My dad and stepmother were at the kitchen table playing Christian "Poker" (you know, ROOK?). We three kids were in the back bedroom with their three children playing Monopoly.

My glass of cola was empty, so I was walking down the hallway toward the kitchen for a refill when I heard the last part of what must have been a response to a question from one of my folks: "Hell no, I don't believe it!" the priest said, "But I preach it anyway, because they need to hear it." I froze in my tracks. I can remember the color rising in my face, and I could feel the heat of it. It wasn't anger…strangely, it was embarrassment. It was as if I had walked in on someone's nakedness but they had not noticed. As I quietly retreated back down the hallway, my fourteen-year-old mind was reeling. As an Eagle Scout I had just completed what the scouting program called the God and Country Award. It had required that I spend nearly two years under the tutelage of my Episcopal priest. It wasn't the cursing that so shocked me, but the inconsistency of his private life with his public image.

From that moment to the day I made Jesus the Lord of my life I had to fight cynicism. The good result of that experience, though, has been a constant self-assessment of my own motives. The last thing I want to find myself guilty of is that hypocrisy I find so repulsive in others.

We are all the sum of the various inputs we receive in life. Sometimes we can control those exposures…and when we can, we should "think on these things" (Philippians 4:8) …but when we cannot, we must be "bringing into captivity every thought to the obedience of Christ" (2 Corinthians 10:5).

Lord, grant my children the avenues of nourishment for their whole persons, which ensure the quality of content they will need for the special tasks to which You have uniquely appointed them. Amen.

FOR ADDITIONAL READING: 1 PETER 2:1; ROMANS 12:9

Six

On the Far Side is Glory

To get something started requires twice the effort it takes to keep it going,
but keeping something going is not possible without any effort at all.

To imagine a thing is grand and glorious,
But to do it is much too laborious,
For most dreamer's dreams grow pale, then fail,
While few e'er result victorious.

What separates victory from defeat?
Why run from those we chase to meet?
For fear of failure or of sure success
We stop short and ne'er complete.

It's 'round the next bend we'll make discover,
In the last chapter we finally uncover;
Think not for a moment an apparent loss
Is anything we'll not soon recover.

Remember the effort we expended at first
The desire for the end that made us thirst
And plow to the far side of the field
Where hidden glory is finally revealed
And dream bubbles cannot be burst.

Dear Lord, make my children to be finishers and not starters only. Let not their euphoria at having started a good thing blind them to the commitment and effort that will be required to bring it to completion. Amen.

FOR ADDITIONAL READING: HEBREWS 12:2-12; JOHN 19:30

SEVEN

Oops. . .Sorry!

There is a right way and a wrong way to do everything.
If you don't have the time to do it right, when
will you have time to do it over?

One bright and cheery, breezy morn,
Over against the hillside lay
Picketed lines of clothes now shorn,
Strewn by gusts in wrinkled array.

Opening the window she glanced out back
Only to find her work undone;
Picking up the full clothespin sack
She wondered where her daughter had gone.

Out in the yard a lone towel muttered
On the line it's terry cloth flapped;
Positioned against the post it fluttered,
Shredded by nails that kept it wrapped.

Oblivious to her Mother's distress
Or caring much for ought but play,
Picking her way through the scattered mess
She ran down the hill and into the fray.

"Oh you, child!" Her mother sighed.
"Once your chore was to hang them out,
Put on clothespins till they dried,
Sort them, fold them and lay them out."

"So now because you didn't do right
Or take the time you should have,
Rewash those clothes till all are white,
Rehang them like you could have.
You'll finish if it takes all night!"

Jesus, let my children take pleasure in a job well done. Let them see the value of excellence and Your worthiness of their best effort every time. Amen.

<small>FOR ADDITIONAL READING: COLOSSIANS 3:23; PROVERBS 14:12</small>

EIGHT

Fickle Flatt'ries' Fare

Everyone is endowed with different gifts from their Creator.
No one has every gift.
No one has no gift.

The only way I can describe how I felt is to say that I had "mixed emotions". You, my sons, would have felt the same way. Everyone came. It was the awards ceremony just before graduation. Imagine watching all the jocks swaggering forward when their names were called to receive their football and basketball trophies and then walking forward yourself to receive your own glorious due…the Elizabeth Cosgrove Poetry Cup! If only I could have made myself invisible. The snickers and jeers were almost unbearable.

Was I ashamed? Not exactly. It was closer to *abject humiliation!* Could I ever live that down? (Perhaps, subconsciously, that is why I have never attended a high school reunion.) Yet, I was proud, in a way, of my accomplishment.

When I was in the seventh grade, I showed up for basketball team try outs; the coach must have had a good laugh. Before I could even get onto the court he took one look at my 4'11" frame and said I needed to "gain a little more experience." How was I to get the experience if I couldn't play on the team?

And yet, where are all those athletic trophies today? The ones that haven't been lost in a move are tarnishing in a forgotten box or gathering dust in a closet. But the gift that God gave me for expressing myself in a literary fashion is, I pray, blessing you even now. I didn't have the maturity then not to envy those athletes whose exploits I could never match. And perhaps it is too much to ask to think that you wouldn't desire what others so greatly admire. So please remember this:

> The seat of honor, do not trust,
> Though gifts have placed you there,
> For those who praise, may poison serve,
> 'Tis fickle flatt'ries' fare.

Lord, help my children identify their gifts and use them for Your glory. And may they see the gifts that others possess without envy, rejoicing at Your providence. Amen.

FOR ADDITIONAL READING: PROVERBS 18:16

Nine

Heroes and Victims

My children, you will rise or fall with the company you keep;
choose wisely those you would befriend, but
seek not those who think themselves generous befriending you.

When I was nine or ten, there was a boy of thirteen (I'll call him Robert) in our neighborhood that I idolized. Robert lived just three doors down and was the coolest guy in the entire universe. He had the fastest bike and the most freedom of anyone I knew. Everyone wanted to be his friend, but I knew I was his best friend…I mean I had to be because sometimes he would even wave back when I hollered at him across the back yards between us.

One Fourth of July weekend I came home with a sack full of fireworks that I didn't have the money to buy. When my dad asked me where I had gotten them, I told him that Robert had bought them for me. My dad had that gift God gives all fathers in some measure…he knew I was not telling the whole truth. You see, I was a good liar (perhaps I should say skillful; a "good" liar is an oxymoron—there is nothing moral about prevaricating), and I knew to salt my lie with half-truths to make it believable…it just never worked with your grandfather. He finally got me to confess that I had helped watch while Robert stole the fireworks from an undermanned stand. After disciplining me, he made me take back the sack and pay for it. Then he told me to leave the fireworks behind, too. He said something to me that I am glad I took to heart. "Son, he is no friend who helps you sin. You are not to go anywhere with Robert again. Do you understand?" I nodded my head as vigorously as I rubbed my behind ruefully.

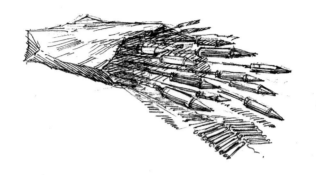

Six years later, while trying to impress some of his young friends, Robert pointed what he thought to be an unloaded gun at his seventeen-year-old sister and killed her. She was only a few months from graduation. It was a tragedy that shook our small town to the core and made me realize the wisdom of my father's counsel.

God, grant my children the ability to discern a flattering tongue. Amen.

FOR ADDITIONAL READING: ROMANS 12:16

TEN

A Sure Defense

Good reputation has its basis not in
what men think about you, but in what God thinks.
Men will eventually adopt God's viewpoint on the matter…
willingly or unwillingly.

Your Mother told me of an experience she had before I met her. I remember how impressed I was at the level of maturity she must have possessed. It happened that Lynn had managed to secure a ride home for Thanksgiving break along with several other students, each of whom would be dropped off en route. A young man I'll call Stanley had offered his car for transportation, and Lynn had offered him Thanksgiving dinner at her house in Massachusetts as a way of saying thanks. Getting sick with the flu, Lynn was not able to make the trip back on the appointed day, so the other students caught flights back to college while Stanley waited to take a less nauseated Lynn a day later.

After a wreck in New York, speedy repairs, and a long, slow journey in a now-rickety car, Stanley suggested that they stop and get a motel room. Lynn thought he meant for them *each* to get one but she didn't have the money for hers. With many reassurances and every impression given to this point that he was a perfect gentleman, she consented to take the bed and he took the floor with a pillow and blanket. She didn't know how long the lights had been out when he tried to make advances on her, but she ran out the door, glad she had decided to sleep fully clothed. Without so much as an apology or even a word to ease the tension, Stanley drove Lynn the remainder of the way.

Before long, Lynn was approached by some of her friends who asked if Stanley was telling the truth about Lynn's escapades with him. Apparently he had created in his imagination the sordid details that would avenge the rejection he had suffered. Tempted to defend herself with the accurate version, which might have resulted in Stanley's expulsion from the college, she felt a check in her spirit. Instead, she merely told them that his version was purely fictional.

Lynn explained, as she shared with me later, that the Lord had said to her, "I will defend you. If you defend yourself that will be the only defense you will have." A few weeks after returning from Christmas Break, Stanley was suspended from college for other offenses not entirely dissimilar. Many who had heard about Lynn's experience came to her saying, "I never doubted you for a moment."

When it is one person's word against the other, two things are indispensable supports: Truth which stands the test of time *and* allowing the Lord to render justice.

Lord, while it is my desire that my children maintain a reputation that is above reproach, never let them be sidetracked by the opinions of others at the cost of their integrity with You, but let them rather trust in your eventual vindication of their Godly acts. Amen.

FOR ADDITIONAL READING: PROVERBS 12:19

ELEVEN

The Taste of Triumph

*Every young person should endeavor to learn a team sport
and an individual sport.
Interdependence, friendship, cooperation, and trust come by the one;
patience, self-confidence, diligence, and humility by the other.*

I guess my favorite candy of all is the apple-flavored Jolly Rancher. I love them to this day (and I should be long past the age of craving sweets) because they take me back to some of my fondest memories. The minute I taste that tart apple flavor I am on the baseball diamond playing shortstop in Pee Wee league. Every boy in my neighborhood played ball and knew the essential benefits of a bulge in your cheek. You just couldn't be as coordinated without chewing a huge wad of gum or sucking on a Jolly Rancher.

At eight years of age I was pretty small, but my Dad helped me make up for my lack of stature by helping me with my fielding skills. He would grab the gloves and me, and we would play catch for hours in the front yard. He told me of the games he went to when he got to see Mickey Mantle playing minor league in our own town, and I would fantasize about my own heroic exploits. In reality, I don't think our team won a single game in the first two forgettable years I played.

I do remember two games in my third year. The first was our next to last game of the season. We had not won a game all season, but it looked like we might just pull this one off. We had come to the bottom of the seventh inning, which at that age meant the last inning, and the score was tied with two outs. I remember thinking how relieved I was that I was not due to bat. The thought of having that kind of pressure made my stomach churn. Then, before I knew it, the next three batters got on base and it was my turn to bat! As I walked to the plate, my whole world began closing in upon me. The crowd was cheering but I couldn't hear them; my coach patted me on the back and said something encouraging I'm sure, but I was in a daze. How could this happen? To me?

Three strikes later and the numbness began to wear off. I could hear my teammates asking me what happened. I could feel the disappointment in their eyes. I had let them down when they were depending upon me the most. The coach reassured me with some words of comfort, but they fell on deaf ears. My tragic performance had proven what I had known was the truth all along—I should never have tried to play this game! Why had my Father insisted that I try out? He had probably bribed the coach so he would let me play! In fact, I was probably the reason that the team I was on had never won a game…*in three years!*

I would have never shown up for the last game of the season had not my Dad insisted. "Your team is depending on you, Son," he had said. Yeah. Right! But I did show up. With Jolly Rancher firmly implanted in my cheek, I determined that I would give this, my last game before retirement, my best effort.

The game started off well for us. We put a couple of runs on the board early, but the other team answered with three of their own. We got another one in the fourth inning to bring us even, but they came out swinging and took the lead again four to three. Then a miracle occurred; I hit a ball deep to right field and took off like a jackrabbit. My teammate on second scored and I was rounding third when I could tell it was going to be close. The catcher planted himself to guard the bag and I could see from his eyes that the throw was on the way. I dove between his legs just as he placed his mitt in the middle of my back. Had I lost the game for my team again? But wait! The Umpire's hands were outstretched palms down. I was safe!

I cannot describe to you the euphoria that swept over me. There was no time to savor that triumph, however, for the game was not yet over.

The next two times at bat for each team produced nothing and it looked like we were going to coast to our very first victory. We just had three outs separating us from a page in the history books! Then things began to fall apart. Our pitcher walked the first batter. No problem. We'll just get the next three. Then the next batter hit a single sharply to left. The incoming throw to the second basemen was bobbled and when the dust cleared there were runners on second and third and nobody out. Hope was beginning to turn to despair.

They say that every person, before they die, is famous for fifteen minutes. My fifteen minutes was about to begin. The next batter lined the first pitch sharply to my left. I made a diving stab, caught the ball in the end of the web of my glove, somersaulted back to my feet, stepped on second and threw to third for a *triple play!* The crowd went wild! My teammates were swarming me and picking me up on their shoulders and parading around the field! I could have died a happy young man right then and there!

And so goes life. A friend of mine once related to me the summary of his coach's wisdom: "You win some, you lose some, some get rained out; but you suit up for all of them." Or as Rudyard Kipling so eloquently wrote:

> "If you can dream—and not make dreams your master;
> If you can think—and not make thoughts your aim;
> If you can meet with Triumph and Disaster,
> And treat those two impostors just the same…you'll be a Man, my son!"[2]

Lord, let not my children think any more highly of themselves than they ought …nor more lowly. Amen.

FOR ADDITIONAL READING: ROMANS 12:3

TWELVE

The Fifty-Cent Lesson

The ability to learn is directly proportional to the desire to be taught.

I have always liked the concept of an allowance given to kids. I *really* liked it when I was a kid and still like the concept, although I am now the compensator instead of the compensatee. There are many valuable but inexpensive lessons you can learn about money management when you are young. The older you get, the more those lessons cost. I'll give you an example.

When I was eight years old, my brother and I used to go to the Ritz Theater every Saturday for the matinee. In those days you could get into the theater, watch a half-a-dozen cartoons and a double feature, get a box of popcorn and a coke, and enjoy air-conditioned comfort for only a quarter. It was a lot to us, but my parents thought it was a small price to pay for half-a-day of peace.

One particular Saturday morning, I awakened Mark, my brother, a little early. We hurriedly got dressed and slipped out to go bike-riding. My Dad always paid us our allowance on Fridays because that was when he got paid. He would ask us whether or not we had been diligent to do our chores around the house. And we would always respond with a yes, nodding vigorously.

As we rode around we passed a drug store and dismounted to go inside for a candy bar. Since we both had our allowances in our pockets, we decided to go ahead and buy something and forego the popcorn at the movie. Mark's favorite candy bar was the Baby Ruth and mine the Butterfinger. You wouldn't believe how large a nickel candy bar was then! We reasoned that if one candy bar was so good then another would be even better. I don't know how it happened, but before we knew it we had consumed *five* candy bars each. As I rode home, my stomach didn't feel too good and I had a sinking feeling that my Dad was not going to be too pleased with all this. But it was *my* money, I reassured myself, and *I* could spend it any way *I* wanted!

My Dad was in his workshop when we rode up. The screen door creaked. "Boys? Is that you?" he queried. We were almost inside. "Hey! Where are you guys headed in such a hurry? Are you getting ready to go to the matinee?"

"Uh, no sir," I replied, my sudden politeness betraying my guilt. "We were just going inside to get our ball gloves."

"But are you going to go to the matinee later?" he pressed.

"Uh, no sir," I replied, hoping against hope he would just go back to his project.

"You're not? Why is that?" he asked, finally coming out of the workshop to face us on the porch. "You do still have your allowances, don't you? You haven't spent it already have you?" I began wondering if he could smell the chocolate on my breath. "How much do you have left?" he asked matter-of-factly.

"Not much," I offered.

"You didn't spend it all, did you?" His voice began to rise.

"Yes, sir," I returned weakly.

"Well let's see what you bought. Did you get a comic book or a toy?" he asked. "I mean surely you have something to show for your money." I made no response, but my eyes betrayed me, I was certain. "You didn't buy *candy* with that money did you?" I learned later that my mouth and the front of my shirt told him the truth long before he eked it out of me. "What kind did you buy?" he went on.

"Butterfinger," I managed to blurt out. The very sound of that name now filled me with a queasiness I had trouble controlling. And as he pointed to my brother, Mark said proudly through chocolate teeth, "Baby Ruth!" (You have to understand that Mark had been hydrocephalic as a child and had sustained permanent brain damage as a result. His simple mind did not see the error of our actions.)

"You mean to tell me that you spent all twenty-five cents on candy bars?" he asked incredulously. "The same *kind* of candy bar?" I was at a total loss for words and was sure my fate had been sealed anyway. "Well, boys, I guess we need to make another trip to that store." He motioned for us to get in the car, and the sense of dread I had been trying to hide now surfaced in a flushed face. Or was that my blood sugar going crazy?

My Dad marched straight in to the store and up to the candy counter and purchased *ten* Butterfingers and *ten* Baby Ruths. He drove us home silently. When we pulled into the carport he finally said, "Boys, since you like candy so much, you can just sit right here on this porch until you eat every one of these candy bars."

I began to whimper but began unwrapping my first Butterfinger and bit into it. I don't know how much time elapsed before I began my second candy bar, but I had run out of tears and was just feeling overwhelmingly nauseated. It was at that moment that Mark looked over at me and said, "Need some help?" He had eaten every one of his Baby Ruths and was looking hungrily at my remaining pile!

I learned an important lesson that day—the responsibilities of stewardship are not to be taken lightly. It was not a lesson that I particularly wanted to learn at eight years of age, but my Dad sure knew how to create within me an intense desire to learn.

Father, multiply the desire of my children to learn; let their pursuit of knowledge be a pursuit of You; let Your glory, revealed to them, bring them a humility that says, "Oh, Lord, there is so much I have yet to learn." Amen.

FOR ADDITIONAL READING: PROVERBS 12:1

THIRTEEN

Scarlet Letters

True humility is having God's perception of yourself.

My dear and precious children, I have thought long and hard about what I would write to you here as a parable or poem of some event in my life that would underscore the truth of this proverb on humility. First, I wrestled with the possibility of sharing one of the darker abhorrent skeletons in my closet that would shock you into the reality of the abiding vulnerability to which all men are subject. Then I thought that I might do more damage by the revelation of a heretofore secret sin of my past than any good it might yield. And, finally, I have come to the conclusion that the path of greater humility might be to let your imagination conjure up what it may and to admit to whatever evil it would suppose. Surely, "but for the grace of God, there go I."

Shame is a burdensome and wonderful gift of God. Those who have come to the place in their lives where they feel no shame are doomed to spiral ever downward in moral disintegration to destruction. Those who feel nothing but shame have come to the end of themselves and can only be rescued by the loving hand of a merciful God, lifting their downcast eyes to gaze into His…to be lost in His forgiving love and found in His restoring favor. I am in this second group. I, with Paul, can truly say, "Oh, wretched man that I am! Who shall deliver me from the body of this death? I thank God through Jesus Christ our Lord" (Romans 7:24-25).

Shame is burdensome in that I am never more than a memory away from the devastating consequences of the follies of my life. And shame is also a wonderful gift for the same reason. As I reflect on the wretchedness of my sin, I see the magnitude of God's grace and my heart swells with love and resolve. *Love,* because whoever is forgiven much loves much. (Paraphrase, Luke 7:47) And *resolve,* because that kind of forgiveness can only evoke determination to live a life pleasing to God.

Children, remember that there is no repented sin that cannot be washed away by the blood of Christ and that with God, forgiven is forgotten.

Father, as my children see their wretchedness in the mirror of Your perfection, comfort them with Your view of their perfection as seen through the blood of Your Son. Amen.

FOR ADDITIONAL READING: 1 JOHN 1:9; JEREMIAH 31:34; PSALM 103:12

FOURTEEN

This is the Way. . .

Intelligence is the ability to learn, while education is the learning itself.
Proof of having been educated is evidenced by change;
first in the way you think, then in the way you live.
Unfortunately, the world has an abundance of "educated" idiots.

To learn from mistakes, experience shows,
Is the best kind of knowledge acquired;
For when you try to do what you know won't work,
You ne'er get the end you desired.

The world has tried many a solution
To ease its suff'ring and pain,
But each time it tries what has already failed,
More loss occurs, not gain.

Perhaps if we lived for a thousand years
And the aged were regarded as sages,
We could learn from them of flawed designs
And the peace that outlasts the ages.

Surely this was the plan from the start
When God made man eternal
Till Sin crept in and aborted that plan,
Condemning him to the infernal.

The only hope now that exists for us
To avoid the destruction we've earned,
Is restoration of relationship lost
By embracing Him Who was spurned.

For Christ Himself is the Ancient of Days
The ageless Sage we need,
To learn from His ways the lessons of life
By following where e'er He may lead.

Doomed to repeat the mistakes of the past
Are all those who refuse to learn,
For how can they say that they know the way,
When it's the Way that they cannot discern?

Lord, help my children make the most of the minds You have given them. Let them not squander this sacred trust nor regard it lightly, but rather may they dedicate all their mental faculties to the learning of You and the teaching of others. Amen.

FOR ADDITIONAL READING: PROVERBS 3:5-6; 16:25; ISAIAH 55:8-9; JOHN 14:6

FIFTEEN

Paying the Dues of Diligence

The law of sowing and reaping is immutable.
It applies to business as well as elsewhere.
You have to do a lot of work for which you are not paid before
you get paid for a lot of work you didn't do.

I will never forget my first day in the real estate business. I was twenty-four years old and loaded for bear. Each salesperson had what we called "floor duty." This was where you answered the phone and got to keep any new leads generated by those calls or leads from customers who walked in the front door.

I had not been on duty for more than an hour when a broken-down old pickup truck bulging with household furniture and personal belongings pulled up in front of the office, and a weather-worn farmer climbed out. He walked in the front door, reached into the front bib pocket of his overalls, and plopped down a wad of wrinkled hundred dollar bills banded together with a wide red rubber band, the kind you see holding together the leaves of a head of lettuce in the produce section of the supermarket. "I want to buy a house today," he said quite matter-of-factly.

For someone as inexperienced as I was, this event made quite an impression. I thought to myself, "Gee, this is going to be a cinch!" And it was. Three hours later he was signing the contract in our office for a $12,500 home. Granted, it was not a very expensive home, even in 1977, but I ended up making $187.50 for three hours of work and even got paid for it my first week. I was well on my way to the big bucks for sure! It didn't take long, however, for me to realize how rare an occasion that first day's windfall had been. I would make a meager living at real estate sales my first year, but at the cost of much wheel-spinning. I doubt I made minimum wage if you figured it out hourly.

There have been many times when I have worked very hard for two or three weeks with a client only to have them purchase a home through another agent, netting me nothing for my efforts. Then there was the time in 1987 when I had thirteen signed contracts go south on me in a row. Some couldn't get financing, the appraisals came in too low on a couple, and I even had one of the principals die only days from closing on one of those transactions (I learned to never spend the commission until my check cleared the bank).

Today, when I mostly deal with buyers and that on a rare occasion due to my ministry responsibilities, I sometimes earn $5,000 or more on a transaction that involves less than ten total hours of time. But this apparent $500 per hour wage has come after twenty years of experience. It is the reward of patient diligence, earned trustworthiness, and consistent performance. There are too many young people today who bail out of their jobs when they can't immediately possess what their parents have earned over twenty years of sacrifice. They never see their due season because they won't stay in the same field until harvest.

God, may my children have the patience to wait for their due season. Orchestrate the events of their lives providentially to the increase of their wisdom. Amen.

FOR ADDITIONAL READING: MATTHEW 10:22; PROVERBS 23:5, 30:8

SIXTEEN

Diapers and Deception

There is no wisdom inherent in the chronological advance of years.
Rather, maturity comes by learning the lessons of life
from the instructor of experience.

Perhaps it was because I was wearing a Scout Master's uniform and he thought I might still need to do my "good turn" for the day, or perhaps I just looked gullible to him. In any case, while I was tending the back entrance to the showroom floor of the convention auditorium where my troop had been asked to help haul in equipment for area vendors, I was approached for a handout by a street bum who had walked in from the alley.

I knew he was an alcoholic looking for booze money because I've spent more than a little time volunteering and ministering at inner-city missions. There are the legitimately hapless wanderers who genuinely will "work for food." But more often than not, those seeking a handout are not looking for a hand up.

This man was probably in his early forties, although his lifestyle had put more miles on him than his years would seem to indicate. He smelled of alcohol and personal neglect. His hair was unkempt, his hands darkened from their unfamiliarity with soap, and his clothes seemed to be permanent skin grafts.

He began his pitch, "Sir, my wife and little girl are three-and-a-half blocks from here in my car waiting for me to come back with some diapers. We are on our way back home to Florida and I need every cent I have for gas. Could you spare me three dollars for a package of diapers?"

I looked at him a long time without speaking. Then I said, "I'll tell you what I will do. I will pay you three dollars for a few words of wisdom to my Scouts, but I'll only pay for the truth, okay?" He nodded and I called the boys over.

"Boys, I want you to meet a man of great wisdom. He is going to tell you how to avoid the traps of life that will make you lie to anyone in order to get enough money for another bottle of wine."

I don't guess he had expected that, but he cleared his throat a couple of times and choked out through a single tear, "Fellows, don't end up like me. You stay in school; do what your parents tell you to, and maybe you won't have to con honest folks for that next drink." The boys stared at him in surprise; he turned without asking for his money and started to shuffle off. Then thinking better of it, he turned around and stuck out his hand. I paid him his three dollars and gave him directions to the Timothy House, a place just a couple of blocks away where he could get a hot meal.

After relating to my Scouts why I had given him the money, I told them to remember those very expensive words. "Aw, three bucks ain't so much," one of them piped up. "That's true," I admitted, "But thirty years of misery sure is!"

Lord, if there are any lessons my children can learn by revelation, in Your mercy, so be it. Knowing the resistance I have exhibited to such instructions, I can only pray that in this my children will not follow in my footsteps. Amen.

FOR ADDITIONAL READING: PROVERBS 23:20-21, 31-35

SEVENTEEN

Faithfool

Never consider your circumstances a hindrance to the Will of God.

aving transferred against my father's advice from the Air Force
Academy into Oral Roberts University, I had been informed that
I was on my own financially. I knew that the Lord would provide
in some way and had worked hard all summer at a YMCA camp saving
every penny I could to pay for school. When it came time to settle up with
the registrar's office, I found myself with only enough money for one half
of the first semester's costs. I had received a small academic scholarship
and had taken a job at Pizza Hut to make up the difference. Since I could
only work about twenty hours a week, however, I knew I would have to
have some sort of a miracle or I would not even be able to finish the
semester.

As a new student at ORU, I was required to read Dr. Roberts' book *The
Miracle of Seed Faith Giving*. I found the book timely but didn't really
acknowledge the impact it was having on me until I went to a concert one
night with a young lady I will call Carol. It was our first date. *Living Sound*
was a music group made up of current students and alumni of the university, and they had been given permission to perform on campus. At some
time in the middle of the concert, someone got up and made an appeal for
a love offering so that the group could accept an invitation to go on tour
behind the Iron Curtain into Poland.

As soon as the bucket started making its way toward the back of the hall, I began wrestling with myself about how much to give. In my wallet I had fifty-one dollars: two twenties, a ten, and a one. I never considered giving the one dollar bill...what would Carol think? I just didn't know if I should give ten of the only dollars I had to my name when I had such a huge school bill staring me in the face. There just weren't enough hours available at $1.40 per hour to earn the amount before it was due. Then I could hear the words from Oral's book[3], "Give and let God multiply it back to you." I don't know all the details of my own thoughts and emotions, but I do know that when the bucket finally reached me I dumped all my money in it.

Now I would love to maintain that this noble act was born of pure faith, but I am quite sure that if there were any purity at all in it, it was only for a split second. If Carol hadn't been sitting there, I would have immediately gotten up to go to the end of the aisle to make change! What was I thinking of? If my Dad could see me now! He already thought I had gone off the deep end by enrolling in ORU. (He still had the window sticker on his car: "My Son Is a Cadet at the United States Air Force Academy.") The evening ended rather uneventfully since I had just given away the money Carol and I were going to use for snacks afterward.

Two days went by and I began to wonder how I was going to make it to the next payday. I had clothes to wash! Didn't God know that? Then I received a letter from my former employer at the summer camp stating that they had withheld too much in taxes from my checks, and the letter included a refund for $27.50. That was an unexpected relief! Two days after that I got another check in the mail from *my Dad!* He said that he wanted to reimburse me for the expense of my school insurance. The amount was $23.50! I had my fifty-one dollars back, to the penny! Of course after that I began checking my campus mailbox four or five times a day.

A week later, while I was waiting for the elevator down from my dorm room, I saw a face I hadn't seen for five years. "Frank Sullivan! What are you doing here?" I asked incredulously. Frank and I had been friends in elementary school before he moved to McAlester; we had played on opposite tennis teams in a junior high tournament once, but I had lost track of him since then. He went on to fill me in on the details of the "lost years" and I did the same. Finally he asked, "Hey, do you need a job?"

I explained that I already worked flipping pizzas at 51st and Harvard. He said that "La Fiesta Cantina" was next door to that same pizza joint and that they were hiring waiters. I thought to myself that this might just be the way the Lord was going to meet my impending financial need.

After interviewing with the manager there he offered me the position. When I asked him what it paid, he informed me that it was tips only and that I would be required to pay about fifty dollars for the uniform. I thanked him for his time and told him I would think about it. What was there to think about? Why would I turn down a sure $1.40 per hour for a nebulous nothing guarantee? As I was leaving I met Frank coming in to work. "Did you get the job?" he asked. "Yeah," I responded quite unenthusiastically, "If I want it. Say, Frank, how much do you make per hour average in tips, anyway?" "Oh, four or five dollars per hour, I guess," he replied. "You do? Wow!" I wheeled around in the parking lot and dashed back inside. "Excuse me, sir," I said to the manager, "But I think I'll just take that job."

I paid my school bill when it was due and rejoiced in the harvest my seed had garnered in my mere moment of foolish faith.

Dear God, may the difficulties and challenges my children face find their proper perspective in the shadow of Your omnipotence and love. Amen.

FOR ADDITIONAL READING: LUKE 6:38

EIGHTEEN

One Cool Mosquito Repellent

*My children, the only thing about smoking that looks tough is
the alveoli of your lungs.*

I would like to blame it on the Marlboro Man or Joe Camel…why do kids have to try and look "cool" anyway? Some might say that we are pursuing the approval of our peers or parents or anyone we admire. In the final analysis, however, we are simply responding to a God-planted desire deep within us to hear our Creator say, "Well done…" (Matthew 25:21). And, I also believe there is another force that pushes us in that direction. We want to view ourselves as that self-assured, independent individual who is the master of his own destiny…a very strong motivation to the teenager who is struggling to discover who he is. Somehow, the fact that some acts are illegal or notorious or risky makes them more tempting.

When I was sixteen and convinced of my own indestructibility, I tried smoking cigars for a couple of weeks. My first taste came when I was canoeing in Canada with my Scout troop. The guide, who was a twenty-one-year-old bearded Scouter and the coolest guy in the universe, offered me a cigar the first evening we camped. I saw him silhouetted against a twilit sky, sitting on a rocky point that jutted out over the water like a stubborn jaw and puffing large translucent clouds of smoke from a stinky cigar. When I walked up, he pointed to a foggy haze a couple of hundred yards away out over the water that seemed to be advancing toward us slowly. "You see that?" he asked. Without waiting for my response, he went on to explain, "That's the local mosquito population on their way to the cafeteria." He pulled out another cigar, cut the end off and handed it to me. "Here, this will keep 'em away from you," he said as he lit it. I inhaled deeply.

Although I managed to cough only a couple of times, I couldn't keep the tears from rolling down my cheeks. "This is a really good one," I rasped, hoping I looked like an old pro and grateful that the waning light hid the greening pallor of my face. I felt quite safe from the mosquitoes … and the bears. How could anyone smoke or even be around these wretched things, I wondered, as I took another more tentative drag.

"It takes a little getting used to," the guide chuckled lightly. I determined I *would* get used to them…if I lived that long. I guess I smoked seven or eight on the canoe trip and maybe ten or so after I got back to civilization. I didn't like what it did to the taste of my food so I didn't stick with it long, thank God. I suppose there would be fewer young people who would take up smoking if the tobacco companies would tell more of the other side of the story—perhaps a TV commercial fading out from a gorgeous blond on a sailboat and fading into some cancer-ridden patient taking a drag through a tracheotomy. But there is too much money in the sale of tobacco for that to happen.

Lord, may my children have the wisdom to never begin an abuse of their bodies through any addictive substance. Grant that they have the strength of character that can resist the pressures to conform to this world, and that they rather seek the approval that only Your smile can provide. Amen.

FOR ADDITIONAL READING: ROMANS 12:1-2

NINETEEN

Knowing Who Is Knowing Why

The more you learn, the more you have left to learn.
You can either get depressed with that fact or you can rejoice
that your wonderful pursuit of knowledge and
understanding will never come to an end.

Perhaps it was because your grandfather, Ray Sargent, was an amateur inventor, or perhaps it was because my junior high biology teacher, Mrs. King, took such a personal interest in my scientific curiosity; in either case, I developed at a very early age an intense desire to understand the laws of nature and the cosmos. My very first Science Fair project won a NASA award and an all-expense paid trip to study at the Manned Spacecraft Center in Houston, Texas, with fifty other kids from around the nation. That was a pretty heady experience for an eighth grader. Although it was only for a week, and no doubt provided more public relations value than real education, I took it seriously and determined right then to pursue the path to "astronaut-hood."

This experience also led to further quasi-scientific experimentation on my own, as it might be argued that teenage science may lack empirical credibility. Still, I am sure I made up in enthusiasm and imagination what I may have lacked in expertise. When I was a sophomore, I began working on a research paper in conjunction with a Science Fair project on the same subject: "The Quest for Extraterrestrial Life."

In my project I created a chamber where I could simulate a Martian atmosphere. It included the right proportions of gases, limited lighting, and maintained the frigid temperature of the surface environment by way of liquid nitrogen. In this chamber I placed Petri dishes of various bacterial strains in agar to determine their viability in such a hostile environment.

I even wrote one of my heroes, Dr. Carl Sagan, whose address I had secured from the National Geographic Society, and asked him for some of his views on the possibility of life outside Earth's environs. It was a great thrill to get a hand-signed personal letter from him.

You might ask how it is that I did not become a research scientist or an astronaut but rather a Bible teacher in a tiny Christian college in Arkansas. In my view, however, I have never really departed from my pursuit of the unknown. I still have great curiosity about the laws of nature, but I find that the key to understanding them is to understand nature's God. I firmly believe today, in what many describe as a post-Christian America, that much scientific progress is being impeded by the refusal to acknowledge the truths our Founding Fathers considered "self-evident."[4] They understood the harmony between "the laws of Nature and of Nature's God."[5]

Is there an E.T. out there somewhere anxious to establish a relationship with a young lad who loves Reese's Pieces? For theological reasons I shall explain to you sometime, I doubt it. There is, however, a T.E., a Terrestrial Emmanuel, a God who came to earth. And, yes, He does want to establish a relationship with anyone who loves Him.

I still have a zillion questions about you name it and most of them start with "Why?" But I have come to this understanding: knowing Who is knowing why.

MY CHILDREN, THE PURSUIT OF KNOWLEDGE IS, AFTER ALL,
THE PURSUIT OF GOD.

May my children love learning but not so much that they cease to apply their knowledge in the building of a Godly society. Amen.

FOR ADDITIONAL READING: PROVERBS 16:18-25; ROMANS 1:18-20

TWENTY

The Responsibility of Relationships

In relationships, there is just no substitute for time spent together.
How can you be close friends with someone
to whom you've never been close?

We live in a day and time when people pay for everything. If you need your house painted, you call the painter; if you need your dryer fixed, you call the appliance repairman; if you need your car towed, you call the wrecker service; if you need your children looked after, you call a babysitter. Compare notes with the elderly and you will find that this was not always so.

In those nearly forgotten days of yore, if you needed something done, you called on your neighbor. Someone in the neighborhood could paint, or fix appliances, or had a tow-bar, or would gladly watch your kids. The neighbors knew that you would soon be returning the favor. No one kept score of course, for everyone just knew that things would balance out. Today, we have no idea who our neighbors are, let alone what skills they might possess. We haven't spent time with them, so we don't feel it would be appropriate to ask them to do anything for us. We wouldn't think of borrowing their posthole digger or crowbar; we don't know them well enough to borrow, so we just go out and buy one of our own for that once-in-five-year's task that requires a unique tool.

After your Mother and I had lived in San Diego for three years, we decided to move to Arkansas. We backed in the moving van we had rented and loaded all day. As I was pulling down the sliding door to close up the truck, I heard someone walking up behind me. I turned to see an out-stretched hand. "Hello, neighbor," he saluted. "I figured I ought to come over and at least say goodbye before you pulled out." He had lived next door for almost a year and I had never even laid eyes on him before! It was as much my fault as his. We were both so busy attending to the business of our lives that we hadn't taken the time to be neighborly.

Everywhere we look in our culture today there is evidence of a burgeoning relationship vacuum. People's basic needs for intimacy are not being met by meaningful relationships. They desperately delve into delusional relationships—a string of one-night stands—that only leaves them progressively more empty. And it is in the very temporality of those relationships that we find the cause and cure. We just have to take the time for relationships to develop. We must "unbusy" ourselves. No wonder you have to call a wrecker when you're on the side of the road and your car won't start. Everybody is just too busy to pull over and help. You can see it in their eyes sometimes, that look of helplessness as they drive by that says, "I would stop but I'm late already."

Whether it is intimacy with God, your spouse, your children or your neighbor that you seek, it just cannot happen unless you slow down and take time. Sometimes you have to decrease your responsibilities to increase your response-ability.

As the Great Friend, Lord, grant that my children would make time for the development of their relationships with You and with those whom You should ordain. Amen.

For additional reading: Proverbs 14:21; 17:17

TWENTY-ONE

Follow Me

*A good leader never asks those who follow to do any task that
he or she has not done or is unwilling to do.*

If you are lost and lonely,
And cannot find your way;
If uncertainty rules your mind
And logic's lost its sway:
Follow Me.

If questions are too many,
And answers much too few;
If pondering has you weary,
And you haven't got a clue:
Follow Me.

For I am meek and lowly,
I've traversed the lowest part,
I've been where none would venture,
And that without a chart.

I've soared the highest heaven,
Reached heights no one attains,
And done it all in virtue
Hailed by angelic strains.

There is no place on earth
Or abysmal depths below
Where My shadow has not fallen
As I've led in radiant glow.

So when you are despairing
And cannot see the shore,
Remember I will not lead you
Where I've not been before:
Follow Me.

Heavenly Father, as you sent your Son into this world to give the command, "Follow Me," (Matthew 16:24) so let my children lead by example; and grant, Lord, that their example may be glorifying to You. Amen.

FOR ADDITIONAL READING: JOHN 12:26; 2 TIMOTHY 2:1-4

TWENTY-TWO

20-20 Hindsight

Never risk what you cannot afford to lose.

A ll decisions involve some risk assessment. You have to weigh what is to be gained with what may be lost if you fail. Sometimes you may decide that there is simply not enough potential gain for the risk.

Let me give you a couple of examples that will serve to underscore my advice here. Many times I have been in a hurry to get somewhere and have streaked past a slow-moving vehicle on a narrow road, speeding to get back in before the end of the passing zone only to find, ten miles down the road, that same car slowly pull up behind me at the traffic signal! I risked an accident, the lives of the occupants of the other car and my own, my insurance rates, and a reckless driving citation to gain what? A thirty-second advantage? It just isn't worth it.

Another potential wreck I narrowly averted taught me a lesson in risk assessment that I shall never forget. I had been "seeing" your mother for about two months when I got the bright idea to ask out another girl. (I put the word "seeing" in quotes because it is a nondescript way of qualifying a relationship; I didn't really know how I felt about Lynn. She was rapidly becoming a great friend and I had been spending copious quantities of time with her, but we had yet to have one of those defining-moment conversations that are so essential to a relationship if it is to go somewhere.)

At that time at Oral Roberts University, as is true at many Christian colleges today, the women vastly outnumbered the men. I had been attracted to a very cute and talented young lady for some time, admiring her at a distance…fantasizing about my chances with someone so obviously desirable as she saying yes to someone so obviously beneath her social strata as I. Perhaps I had gained sufficient confidence through my friendship with Lynn that I had finally conjured up the necessary courage…in any case, I asked her to go to a campus basketball game and, to my amazement, she accepted!

The game is a blur in my memory. I don't remember whom we played or who won. I do remember the date though. I had a great time with Kathy, but I have to admit that I was pretty uncomfortable. It wasn't my date that made me that way but rather the fact that Lynn was sitting only a couple of rows back and a few seats over. I remember reasoning with myself at the time…Lynn and I didn't have a commitment to each other that went beyond friends; so why was I feeling like such a jerk?! I wondered if she were going to be miffed at me for this, but I didn't have to wonder long.

When I called Lynn the next day, her roommate answered the phone and responded quite icily that Lynn was too busy to come to the phone. All subsequent calls for nearly a week received the same treatment. Obviously, we were having that defining-moment conversation…non-verbally! And it was up to me to make a choice. I weighed the richness of my relationship with my best friend and the rapidly awakening feelings I was having for her with what might or might not happen with Kathy Lee. The decision was pretty easy.

When I called Lynn the next time, I told her roommate that I had something to say to Lynn if she would listen, but this was going to be my last call if she would not. When Lynn came to the phone, I did what anyone else in my shoes would have done … I threw myself on her mercy and begged her forgiveness. I had decided that what was to be gained with Kathy Lee was not worth the risk of my future with Lynn, even if that future were as yet uncertain. The rest is, as they say, history. And it doesn't matter either that Kathy Lee Epstein is today Mrs. Frank Gifford. I won the prize in marrying Lynn…and I am sure I'll get no argument from her offspring!

Children, I shall list for you here four things that I have found that you cannot afford to lose … and therefore cannot afford to risk:

1. The favor of God
2. Your family
3. Your good name
4. Your freedom

Lord, grant my children the courage to risk loss for the hope of gain, for so You gave Your life; but grant them also that wisdom to cherish what cannot be replaced. Amen.

FOR ADDITIONAL READING: LUKE 14:28-33

TWENTY-THREE

Horn Hill

Think before you act!
Davy Crockett once said, "Be always sure you're right then go ahead."[6]
This simple advice means to me: Don't proceed until you're sure
that you are right; and once you are certain, don't hesitate.

The skateboard was not invented by a time-traveler trying to escape bullies in a town-square chase in 1955, as the movie Back to the Future might propose, but I was one of the first in my neighborhood in 1963 who had one. They weren't the hi-tech fiberglass models with wide-track polystyrene wheels you see now. Nope, these beauties were usually home-made contraptions constructed from a piece of scrap pine one-by-six and two pair of narrow steel wheels scavenged from a discarded shoe skate.

I remember creating slalom courses, first on my driveway with chunks of rock and later on the asphalt streets with tin cans. One of my favorite innovations was the "Olympic ski run." This sport was a two-man event where the boat-end of a ski rope was tied to a bicycle and the skateboarder held on to the skier-end for dear life.

Being the first in my neighborhood to have a skateboard created a certain obligation, of course, to maintain a skill level that greatly surpassed my peers. Not being very good at any of the really "cool" sports most of my friends excelled in, I was doubly compelled to dazzle and impress. Every time I would try something new, my more agile fellows would soon master it beyond my abilities, and I would have to one-up them to maintain my "edge" (most foolish stunts are usually born from such pre-adolescent philosophies).

Horn Hill, as we liked to call it, was the right-of-passage journey for all elementary-age bicyclers in the neighborhood. It was so steep you could coast for three blocks . . . and that from a standstill! No one had ever even thought about attempting it on a skateboard, for that would have been suicide. But, when the pressure to retain pedestal status became too great, the idea leapt into my mind like a careening race car. Wow! Wouldn't that be just too cool!

There was the necessary risk assessment that must be done, of course, but the indestructibility of youth gave little thought to potential bodily harm. It was, rather, the reputation that was at stake. The risk of failure or of changing my mind at the last minute motivated me to decide to conduct an unannounced private trial run.

As I stood near the right-hand curb at the top of Horn Hill, my skateboard confidently tucked under my left arm like a businessman carrying the morning paper, I surveyed the scene of future glory. I picked out a critical path I thought would maintain a controllable speed and placed the skateboard down on the concrete with a double-clack. Left foot forward on the skateboard, I shoved off with the right...a tenuous push that betrayed a growing anxiety. Too late now, I rapidly picked up speed. Each expansion joint in the roadway jarred my legs, which the vibration had already turned to rubber. I could feel myself losing control. In a desperate attempt to bail out, I steered toward the left-hand side of the street and the beckoning plush green lawn just beyond the curb. But it was not to be. Two feet short of the curb and about to break the sound barrier, I hit the tiny gravel minefield that accumulates near the gutters and was immediately airborne. For a split surreal second I was above the Earth glancing back at my pilotless skateboard like Alan Shepherd gazed at our retreating planet from the Mercury capsule. Then came the impact. I splashed down alright, but my headlong slide down thirty feet of concrete curb and gutter brought me no sense of relief at journey's end.

I picked myself up feebly and just caught a glimpse of an awestruck young idolizer. Suddenly laughing, I picked up the scarred skateboard and began the painful climb back up Horn Hill. I can't say whether it was shock, adrenaline, or pride that got me up that road and back home, but none of that was there to help as I stood under the shower, picked out gravel from the abrasions and noisily released many repressed expressions of agony.

I had a new respect for Horn Hill, and the words of my father still ring in my ear, "Son, think before you act!"

Lord, You know a young person has both the impetuousness of youth and the timidity of inexperience. I pray that You will help my children to plainly see the course before them and replace their natural tendencies with patience and courage. Amen.

FOR ADDITIONAL READING: GALATIANS 5:22; JAMES 1:2

TWENTY-FOUR

When You've Got To Go...

When you want someone to give you his time,
set up an appointment; and always take five minutes less of his time
than he promised. In so doing, you have esteemed him
more highly than yourself.

I t has been said that one definition for the word "punctuality" is show-
ing high esteem for others and their time. And, in this regard, the only
thing I can think of that is more disrespectful than tardiness is walking
away while someone is speaking to you.

When I first began attending Oral Roberts University in 1971, chapel
was conducted on the top floor of the Learning Resources Center. On
numerous occasions I had the privilege of hearing Oral Roberts personally
address the student body, and I was always intrigued by his charisma and
his command of the audience. Although there were often students who
rudely spent their chapel time working on assignments for their next
classes, few rarely just got up and walked out. Even when that did occur,
their quiet and careful deportment suggested they were departing for
some previously arranged appointment. They usually sat near the rear of
the auditorium and left quite unobtrusively.

One particular morning though, the administration, having apparently felt these departures might be getting out of hand, decided to nip it
in the bud. Dr. Carl Hamilton took part of the announcement portion of
the service to sternly remind the students to show proper respect for their
speakers and not depart before the end of chapel. Things proceeded
smoothly until about ten minutes into President Roberts' message.

Suddenly, a young lady seated about five rows from the front stood up and proceeded to make for the aisle, stumbling and tripping over the legs of her surprised classmates. She made such a commotion in her exit that President Roberts looked up at her and motioned Dr. Hamilton to follow. I remember feeling sorry for the girl as I saw Dean Hamilton walk off the platform and pick up the pace of his pursuit.

A few minutes later Dr. Hamilton quietly returned to his seat on the dais. Noticing he had returned, President Roberts stopped in mid-sentence and motioned for Dr. Hamilton. Dr. Hamilton approached the lectern and whispered something in President Robert's ear. As he slowly turned back toward the audience, all could see that Oral was processing what he had heard. Then, with a simple shrug, he said to all of us, "When you've got to go, you've got to go." The ensuing laughter soon engulfed the entire auditorium and President Roberts' "famous" words were forever emblazoned into my memory.

Father, grant my children a true humility and a genuine respect of others' time and their opinions. Amen.

For additional reading: Romans 12:10; 13:1-7

TWENTY-FIVE

A Timely Investment

*Show me a man's greatest possession, and
I'll show you what possesses him.*

I t has been said that to discover a man's value system one only need look in his checkbook. That is generally true and a practical demonstration of a biblical principle. The Scripture says, "For where your treasure is, there will your heart be also" (Matthew 6:21).

My Dad and I were walking the back way from your great-grandmother Sargent's house and down an alley behind the rent house we were living in at the time. We happened by the next-door-neighbor's garage to find him carefully buffing out a small scratch on the otherwise flawless paint job he had just put on his 1955 Chevy Sport Coupe. He looked up with a frown as I said, "Howdy," quite cheerily. I had never met the man, but my father whispered in my ear, "Our neighbor's not too friendly, but watch this."

"That has to be the most gorgeous piece of steel and glass I have ever seen!" my Dad exclaimed.

The neighbor glanced up from his work skeptically, but my father's apparently sincere appreciation made his scowl disappear into a sheepish grin. "Really? You think so?" he responded. And then he was off into a fifteen minute discourse on how he had come across the car originally, what work he had done on it himself, and how he loved to drive it slowly around town on Sunday afternoons and wave acknowledgingly to admirers.

After we managed to pry ourselves away, I asked my Dad how he had known what our neighbor's response was going to be. "Son," he said, "I have seen this man tinkering on this car for months…washing, waxing, polishing…and anyone who invests that kind of time on anything must value it highly. When I showed regard for what he valued, he just couldn't help but value me."

I have learned many valuable lessons from my father; some by the good things he showed me, some by the things we did together, and some by the mistakes I saw him make. But by his willingness to spend time to teach me how he believed the world worked, he showed me how much he valued me. My children, never underestimate the value of the time you spend with those you love.

Lord Jesus, may you be both Possessor and possession of my children. Amen.

FOR ADDITIONAL READING: 1 TIMOTHY 6:10; 1 JOHN 2:15-17

TWENTY-SIX

Gum, Guts and God

They say that the proof is in the pudding.
The proof of desire is in pursuit.

I shall never forget my eighteenth birthday. When I left home for the Air Force Academy on June 29th of 1970, I knew I had finally achieved what I had worked so long and hard for during the previous several years. I can't really remember when I first conceived of the idea to be an astronaut…it had to be sometime in the spring of 1962 after John Glenn made his historic orbital flight in *Friendship 7*. He and the other six heroes of NASA's Mercury Space Program were out to change their world. I remember my nine-year-old mind racing with possibilities that following summer and many summers after as I devoured every piece of science fiction I could get my hands on. I read Heinlein, Bradbury and Asimov, and even Jules Verne; I couldn't get enough of time travel or space exploration or intergalactic adventure.

I had a gift for math and the sciences and paid no attention to the nerd-slurs my belt-clipped slide rule invited. I entered every science fair from eighth grade upwards and worked hard at physical conditioning, especially as I entered my senior year and began competing for an appointment to one of the service academies. When I received nominations to the Naval Academy, the Coast Guard Academy and the Air Force Academy, it was a simple choice for me. I wanted to fly…really high!

Since my birthday was on August 14th, I was only seventeen when I began Basic Cadet Training (BCT) in the summer of 1970. As luck would have it, my squadron was the last to go through the part of BCT that was survival training…and I'm referring to *bad* luck. The training was held in Saylor ("nosebleed") Park in the Rampart Range of the Rockies just behind and somewhat vertical from the Academy itself. We had trained in the "lowlands" all summer at a mere 7,250 feet above sea level, but the final part was to try and survive at a rarefied 10,000 feet plus altitude, foraging over areas where every spare root and bug had already been ravenously consumed by our fellow, but previous, sufferers.

Our upper class trainers taught us how to make squirrel traps from wire, deadfall traps from rocks, sticks and nylon parachute chord; and the area fauna were well amused, I'm sure. About the third day into our week-long forced fast, our evening campfire conversation turned from the girls we'd left at home to "what I wouldn't give for a Big Mac." I thought I couldn't drink one more cup of wild strawberry leaf tea when one of our training officers drove up with a cage full of live rabbits. Following our instruction in the fine art of painless rabbit execution, we began preparing rabbit stew, roasted rabbit, rabbit-on-a-stick, and other hare-fare. The next day began a series of twenty miles-per-day forced marches that brought me to the brink of a "whose-brilliant-idea-was-this-anyway" line of reflection.

As we faced the last hill on our third and next-to-last day of marches, I breathlessly remarked to one of my G-Squadron (we had adopted the name "Guts Squadron") fellow cadets, "Hey…guess what. It's my birthday. What a way to spend my eighteenth birthday!"

A moment later, a well-fed and jubilant upperclassman stepped to the front and said, "Okay, let's show 'em what we're made of. The only way to take the last hill is at a dead run!" And he led the charge up the last three hundred yards to our various positions of gasping collapses. When I finally caught my breath and the pain in my chest was beginning to sub-side, I looked up to that same cadet, who alone knew it was my birthday, offering me the greatest gift I have ever gotten on any birthday before or since: one stick of Juicy Fruit chewing gum! He had managed to smuggle a pack on our trek and had only one piece left…and *he gave it to me!* That was the best piece of gum I have ever chewed…and chewed…and chewed.

I remember thanking God for the generosity of that fellow cadet, whose name, for some reason, I have forgotten, along with much else I'm sure I've repressed of those experiences. (Wherever you are, my friend and brother, may God multiply back to you once again your sacrificial gift to me that day.) I remember, too, the "stick-to-it-tiveness" the Lord gave me that enabled me to finish survival training and the rest of BCT. And, although I would later exchange my dreams of becoming an astronaut for entering the ministry, I did not perceive that as a change in direction, but only a change of vehicles. I still want to change the world and have pursued that goal with everything within me. If you want something badly enough, you will find a way to pay the price to obtain it.

Lord Jesus, as You would not be swayed from the painful path that was set before you, so let not my children shrink back from the difficulties of life and so miss the reward of accomplishment. Rather grant that their pursuits might reflect those Godly desires which you have planted deep within them. Amen.

FOR ADDITIONAL READING: ROMANS 5:3-4; JAMES 1:3-4

TWENTY-SEVEN

Blood on Our Hands

*When you let the enemy paralyze your potential through fear, he
will "peril-ize" your walk with God.*

Dave Cerullo and I met under unique circumstances. I had
needed a ride from Tulsa to Stillwater where I could catch
another ride down to minister at a youth retreat in Waco,
Texas. Rick, a friend I had met when we both were Y-Camp counselors,
was a student at OSU and had offered to get me to Waco if I could get to
Stillwater. I had posted a "Need-A-Ride" note on the bulletin boards in the
dorms at ORU and Dave, who drove from ORU to Stillwater weekly to
visit his fiancée, Barb, offered to give me a ride. An hour-and-a half long
ride later, Dave and I had become friends. Six months later still and I was
driving out to San Diego to go to work for his father, an international
evangelist.

Dave had learned some difficult but important lessons as the son of a
well-known minister of the Gospel. One of those lessons he shared with
me one afternoon after we had finished snorkeling in La Jolla Cove.
Although the twenty-odd years that have elapsed since then may have
altered a detail or two of my recollection of that story, the gist of it remains
powerfully poignant.

Dave had "grown up a Christian," as many who have been raised in
godly homes might understand. He had made a decision to trust Christ as

his Savior at an early age, but as a teen, much of the truth of his relationship with the Lord was, as yet, untried.

One day a high school friend of his came bounding up to him, "Hey, Dave, guess what happened to me," he exclaimed breathlessly! Without waiting for a response he blurted out, "I got saved last night!"

"Wow! That's great! Welcome to the kingdom, brother!" Dave's congratulatory handshake was received enthusiastically. And then the pumping arm of the new believer slowed as his surprised look became consternation, then anger.

"Brother? You mean you're a Christian, too?" he asked suspiciously.

"Why, sure I am," Dave replied. "You remember vacation Bible school, don't you? I've been a Christian a long time."

"Yeah, I remember vacation Bible school, alright. I also remember my parents' divorce, the drugs, the alcohol…the suicide attempts! Where was your Christianity then?"

"Gee," Dave offered weakly, "I just wasn't sure you were ready for it."

"Wasn't ready?" he responded incredulously. "What were you waiting for anyway, the lowering of my coffin?" After that remark, feeling wounded and betrayed, he wheeled and walked rapidly away muttering to himself, leaving Dave standing there, a sheepish and surprised expression on his face.

Dave looked down in embarrassment and began walking on to his next class when suddenly he noticed the reddish stain that coated the palms of each hand. "What's this red stuff?" he muttered to himself absently.

Later that afternoon, having arrived home from school, Dave hollered, "I'm home, Mom." Walking into the kitchen for a snack and finding her there, he asked, "Mom, have you got anything that'll take this red stuff off?" He rubbed his hands together vigorously as he extended them palms upward for her inspection.

"What are you talking about?" she asked. "I don't see anything on your hands."

Later as Dave was reflecting over the events of the day and feeling tearful remorse at the cowardice of his weak faith, he repented. The Lord comforted him and said, "You shall go where I send you and speak what I tell you…to refuse is to have blood on your hands." At that moment, Dave looked down at his hands through the tears of his humble commitment and watched as the redness faded.

Let my children see all things as possible through You, Oh Lord, never fearing failure, but rather welcoming each challenge for the work of character it shall accomplish regardless of the outcome. Amen.

FOR ADDITIONAL READING: EZEKIEL 33:1-9; 2 TIMOTHY 1:6-8

TWENTY-EIGHT

Truth or Consequences

*It is impossible to believe one way and act another…at least not for long.
Right thinking precedes right action.*

T he dictionary defines a dilemma as "a choice between equally unsatisfactory alternatives." I would say that whoever penned that definition hadn't experienced one for himself. I hardly think "unsatisfactory" is a strong enough word to describe the alternatives I faced one day in my young sixteen-year-old life.

When I was growing up, church attendance was a weekly ritual for all but the hung-over and the infirm. It was an assumption of American life, like everyone singing the national anthem at sporting events or starting the school day with prayer—it's not that everyone consciously chose to do so, but rather that no one ever questioned whether or not it should be so.

My father had lost his first wife (my mother, Marianne) to cancer when I was two and had remarried when I was four. After he married my first stepmother, Betty, the family began attending the Episcopal Church, where she was a devoted participant. From the ages of four to sixteen, my spiritual upbringing would be this and, from my experiences there, I would both suffer and benefit. I went through the standard religious training up through my confirmation by the bishop at age twelve and had come to what I would call a "reverence relationship" with God. I didn't really know Him, but I knew about Him and had yet to question much that I'd been taught.

From my confirmation to the time I was sixteen, I went through a metamorphosis of sorts. Various experiences, including a rapidly deteriorating relationship with my stepmother, contributed to a growing cynicism of things religious. Although I was beginning to question the very existence of God, those who claimed to be his followers were even more suspect. It was at this point that I arrived at my dilemma.

It was a Sunday morning in late August. I had just turned sixteen and was in the midst of a cathartic reverie when I began tuning in to what the priest was saying during the communion service. As a senior acolyte, I had served with the priest in many communion services and knew well the order of service and the words of admonition the priest was now reciting. Somehow that day I listened with new ears to his warning to the parishioners against taking of the elements in an "unworthy manner." In my twelve years as an Episcopalian, I had never seen nor heard of anyone who felt compelled to heed that warning by electing not to receive communion. And then I saw the acolyte on duty that Sunday begin his ritual walk down the center aisle, pausing at each row of pews as a signal for that group to stand and make their way to the altar.

My mind began to race. I somehow knew that I could no longer operate in the lie. If I gave in and went up for communion, I would be betraying my own integrity and possibly even offending the same God who may already be pretty peeved at the rest of the hypocrites. If I didn't stand up and go with the rest of our row, my stepmother sitting next to me would be positively mortified and make my life miserable for who knew how long. And then the acolyte was at our row. The moment of truth had come and my legs were leaden. I just sat there and stared straight ahead as nudge and elbow produced no response from me. Finally, clambering around me with a glare, my stepmother went forward.

After the service, I made myself scarce but knew the ride home would not be pleasant. My stepmother found me in the parking lot and railed at me with angry tears something about that being the most embarrassing moment of her life. I tuned out after a few seconds of the tirade and walked away. My Dad and I had a conversation later that day. You know, the kind of conversation that begins with "As long as you live in this house…" I forged a strategic compromise with him (I think he was beginning his own metamorphosis of another sort…within six months they were divorced) and agreed I would still attend church weekly. "Just let me go where some of my friends go to church," I requested.

A year-and-a-half later I would find final resolution to my dilemma by making the wisest decision of my life: I made Jesus Christ my personal Lord and Savior.

Holy Spirit, lead and guide my children into all truth and so let them glorify God in all they do or say. Amen.

FOR ADDITIONAL READING: PROVERBS23:7; ISAIAH 26:3; ROMANS 8:6

TWENTY-NINE

Roadkill Café

*Patience is the steel forged on the anvil of Character by the hammer of
Adversity. Tools made from that metal will perform lasting works.*

You don't just wake up one morning and say to yourself,
"Hmm…I think I'll just do something really stupid
today…something that will take my entire family through some
really tough times…yeah, that sounds really great; that's just what I'll do!"
No, my children, it isn't that simple and nobody's that stupid…including
the Devil, himself. Temptation begins at the subtle intersection of dissatis-
faction and opportunity. If the enemy didn't make temptation appealing,
no one would fall for it.

I had the world by the tail—only thirty-two and already a million-
aire…at least on paper. I had justified my resigning from the ministry by
arguing to myself that I could be more help to God by giving to His work
than by doing it myself (that logic sounds really lame to me now). When
the fourth monthly bonus check from my new multi-level marketing
enterprise came in at over $10,000, I knew I had "heard from God." I
resigned my position with Terry Law's ministry (*Living Sound,* at the time)
and threw myself headlong into recruiting and training my "downline"
distributors. After starting full-time in January of 1982, I was flying high
by August of 1984.

Then the bottom fell out. Oh, I had a warning or two. First, out of the
clear blue, Bill Basanski, a respected man of God in the Tulsa area with his

own very successful ministry, called me one day and asked if I would meet him for lunch. He said the Lord had given him a word for me. I remember being a little flattered and somewhat mystified, especially when he told me what the Lord had to say. "It's the little foxes that spoil the vine," he said, quoting an Old Testament passage. I politely thanked him for taking his time to give me that admonition, but I didn't comprehend what those words could mean for me.

Then, when I was in Johannesburg, South Africa, preparing to set up a sister marketing company to the one in which I was prospering, I received my second warning. This one was more to the point and not really a warning but rather a pronouncement of what would inevitably come to pass.

Pastor Franz Esterhuizen had picked me up at the airport at 4:00 a.m. that Sunday. A short nap and six hours later I was sitting in the front row of his church as Franz began speaking prophetic words over various members of his congregation. He came and stood in front of me, pointed his finger, and opened his mouth to speak…then suddenly, with a puzzled look on his face, he closed his mouth and moved on down the row. When I asked him after church if the Lord had spoken to him concerning me, he said that He did, but that he was not to share it at that time.

On Monday, just ten minutes before I was to meet with a dozen investors in my new venture, I received a call from the U.S. It was from the home office of the company that would be supplying our products until we could begin manufacturing them in South Africa. Apparently, the owners (two brothers) of the company had gotten in a squabble and had decided to close the doors rather than have each other as enemies.

Now what, I thought. All of those folks back in the U.S. whom I had enrolled were in the same dilemma I was…no product to sell. But there was nothing I could do about it from half-way around the world. I decided to stay the rest of the planned three weeks. Perhaps the brothers would come to their senses, or someone would buy them out. I stayed, visited friends, toured the countryside and waited. Soon, the time of my departure had arrived and I had all but forgotten about the aborted admonition from Franz. Then, on the way to the airport he said, "Well, Brother Alan, the Lord has released me to tell you what I heard Him speak to me that first Sunday you were here."

"Really? And what's that?" I asked.

"He said to tell you that, 'All the props were going to be knocked out from under you and that you were to just wait on Him.'"

Great, I thought! Now what is that supposed to mean? Although I was duly concerned about the disposition of my three product warehouses, the interruption of my commission income, and other related economic concerns, I still was not too worried. I had known that it was imprudent to "put all my eggs in one basket" so to speak, so I had been diversifying my investments; I owned an advertising agency, some oil interests in eastern Colorado, an exclusive marketing arrangement for a new kitchen appliance (a hand-held mixing wand), and 160 acres of land with a mile of shore frontage on Lake Hudson, just minutes outside of Tulsa. In spite of this, everything I touched "went south." The bottom fell out of the oil industry, people I had trusted in business bailed out owing me large sums of money…and by the time the smoke cleared, we had been forced to divest ourselves of everything. The last to go was the lake property. It was the hardest to part with since I had wanted for years to build a summer camp for kids at that location. There was a little consolation in knowing that Willie George (known to thousands of youngsters as "Gospel Bill"), who purchased my property, did so for the purpose of building Camp Dry Gulch. To this day kids are having their lives transformed by the love of God.

Then, on January 2, 1986, less than seventy-two hours after making that sale, Lynn and I were on the road coming back from having spent the holidays with her family in Massachusetts. We had just switched drivers so I could sleep. Suddenly, I awakened to her screaming as our Jeep Wagoneer headed toward a three hundred foot drop-off. I quickly grabbed the steering wheel and jerked it hard to the right. The vehicle did not immediately respond as we were sliding on "black ice." Then, in an instant, the tires caught on a clear portion of asphalt and we went hurtling across the highway, crashing directly into a sheer granite mountain cut.

What transpired from that point you already know…the first day or two of uncertainty for me…the miraculous recovery from what should have been fatal or at least crippling … and the ultimate complete collapse of our family's economic well being. When we moved to Hot Springs, Arkansas, in June of 1986, it was in a very used 1976 Granada automobile your grandmother had purchased for us. We struggled to make the $400.00 per month rent, and there were times when I told your mother I'd be home from the office as soon as the Lord provided gas for the return trip.

It was then (in 1987) that we thought we had "bottomed out," for we had to file for bankruptcy. Oh, did I mention that the wreck had occurred two days after our insurance on the car had expired? Much of what we sought relief from in the bankruptcy were the hospital bills from the accident.

Then it happened—the lowest point. Our family hadn't had a decent meal in a few days and no meat in more than a week (I can still remember the myriad ways you can fix a potato). I was driving home on fumes, as usual; I had just lost my *tenth* real estate transaction in a row (I was to lose three more before my fortunes reversed themselves), and was traveling down Brookhill Ranch Road when I swerved to miss a rabbit in the road. The telltale thud in my right front wheel-well told me my attempt at evasion had not succeeded. Glancing in the rear view mirror, I could see the receding lifeless form of…DINNER! I slammed on the brakes and backed rapidly down the road, stopping with my rear wheels just short of my prize. After examining the rabbit, I was grateful that I had only hit his head, for the remainder seemed well enough intact. I scooped it up and put it in the car with the excitement of a deer hunter coming home on the opening day of the season.

That night the Sargent family had fried rabbit on the table to go with our potatoes.

You might well ask how I came to such a low point in my life, and the answer is simple: by my own stupidity. I made a series of wrong choices and then deceived myself into thinking I was justified in my actions. I could elaborate, but why glorify the devil? Suffice it to say that I had an overactive "justifier." You know the "justifier," don't you? It is that organ of the body that makes everything appear right in your own eyes!

The Scripture states, "The curse causeless shall not come" (Proverbs 26:2). And I had surely given the Lord cause. Tragically, my family had to endure undeserved the hardship and adversity that my own foolishness had brought on me…and that was the hardest discipline I had to receive from the Lord.

The good news is that God forgave me and restored me, even though I deserved no such mercy. He gave me the opportunity to "renew my strength like the eagles, to run and not grow weary, to walk and not faint" (Isaiah 40:31). Ah, but that's another story…

Lord, never let my children be satisfied with the path of least resistance. Amen.

FOR ADDITIONAL READING: TITUS 2:6-8; 3:3-7

THIRTY

Reaching Twenty-One

Success is not in never failing but rather in never giving up.

Ever since I can remember, I have had a great respect for the Scouting program. I grew up as our troop "mascot" and was going on camp-outs with my Scoutmaster Dad and the dozens of boys he taught long before I was old enough to join. I shall never forget the profound desire that our Senior Patrol Leader, John Ashby, planted deep within me. I wanted so much to be like him. Everyone thought he was cool. And that was back when honor, truth, and achievement were "in" and a young man's head could be turned by the colorful array of merit badges slung over another's shoulder.

I could hardly wait to get to First Class Scout so I could start earning some of those merit badges. The Eagle Scout rank required twenty-one such badges, and I soon discovered that each of them required long hours of study and hard work. To a boy of twelve, Eagle appeared far away and fleeing at great speed. That's when my Dad pulled me aside one night after the meeting. I usually helped him clean up the church fellowship hall where we met, and he rewarded me with a soda pop and a game of ping-pong. I had never beaten my Dad but imagined that I was getting closer each time we played.

"Son," he said, "You've kind of quit working on your advancement, haven't you?"

"Yes, sir," I replied sheepishly.

Then, seeming to change the subject, he asked, "What's the nearest you ever came to beating me at ping-pong?"

"Gee, Dad, about eleven points, I guess." I knew exactly the score. It had happened the week before last and was the first time I had gotten into double digits against him, but he had won twenty-one to ten.

"I guess you think you'll never beat me, huh?" He was almost taunting me. "So why do you keep on trying then?"

"I am going to beat you one day!" I defiantly responded. "And I'm going to do it left-handed!" I challenged.

"Then you are going to have to play a lot and lose a lot before that's ever going to happen," he laughed. "Are you sure you like losing enough to get that good?"

"Nope," I said, "But I *hate* losing enough to get that good. No matter how long it takes, I am going to beat you one day." He then proceeded to beat me soundly, as if to prove his point. After the game, as he was turning off the lights to leave he asked, "How are you doing on your merit badges, son?"

A little disappointed that he had returned to this painful subject, I replied weakly, "Not too well, I guess."

"But I thought you wanted to make Eagle Scout one day."

"I do, Dad, but that's a lot of merit badges!"

"Aw, Son, you just don't want it badly enough. If you wanted to make Eagle as badly as you want to beat me at ping-pong, you'd surely have no problem," he offered. "Besides, getting to twenty-one isn't so hard when you're the only one playing," he said, chuckling to himself at the double entendre.

I never did beat your grandfather left-handed, but I did get good enough to beat him regularly right-handed. And, when I got to twenty-one the first time, I knew I would get those twenty-one merit badges eventually, too … and I did.

Just as You have never given up on me, Lord, so grant my children that same tenacity in their pursuits. Amen.

FOR ADDITIONAL READING: HEBREWS 12:1-4; 1 TIMOTHY 6:12

THIRTY-ONE

Skating on Thin Ice

Disappointment is often the result of unrealistic expectations.

Everyone is vulnerable to deception, especially when it involves believing what you want to be true. You ignore the evidence to the contrary because you want to believe more than you want the truth. This is a type of self-deception and often the worst kind, for there is no one else to blame.

In my desire here to warn you from the dangers of unrealistic expectations and their consequences, I have sought to understand why they occur. I believe it is often that we have chosen deliberately to have these expectations because we are wrapped up in a pleasant self-deception. I say pleasant because having these expectations feeds our fantasies…and our egos.

I had met Sue and Linda Lichty while I was a cadet at the Air Force Academy. They and their mom were members of the same church off the base that I attended. (It was difficult getting off base as a Fourth Classmen, so I joined the "Chapel Corps"—those cadets who volunteered to teach a Sunday school class in Colorado Springs.) When it came time for getting a date for the Christmas Ball, I asked Linda to go. I was good friends with the family and spent a couple of Sunday afternoons at their home immersing myself in a dose of a more pleasant reality.

At some point in the spring of my freshman year, when I began making plans to transfer into Oral Roberts University, I let the Lichty's in on my academic intentions and told them all about ORU. I really think it was that one afternoon's discussion that sparked Sue and Linda's idea to attend there, because I was surprised to bump into them the next semester on the ORU campus.

One day, Linda, who had come to ORU with her sister, suggested that we make a trip up to Rockford, Illinois, to visit her friend Janet Lynn. She had met Janet Lynn at the Broadmoor in Colorado where they had trained together on the same ice. Since I had a car and was crazy enough to pack in a trip to the Chicago area and back between my last class on Friday and my first class on Monday, I was invited to drive. Two of my friends, Zahn Martin and Greg Massanari asked to tag along so they could be dropped at their homes en route, Champagne and Chicago respectively.

The moment I met Janet Lynn, I was smitten. Why not? She was cute, vivacious, talented and not full of herself like so many rising star athletes tend to be. She was also a relatively new Christian and quite serious about her growth in the Lord. In one of those moments orchestrated by the Lord, I had an opportunity to pray for her to be filled with the Holy Spirit.

After that whirlwind trip, we began corresponding and calling. I made another journey to see her and the rest of the Olympic hopefuls at Nationals. I met and made friends with many of them and fancied myself as a sort of team chaplain. That year she and Gordy McKellan both won and earned spots on the 1972 Olympics team. And I was more than a little crushed when she broke it off with me…but what did I think was going to happen? She spent eight hours a day, six days a week on the ice …I skate like a big rock on thin ice. I mean, what did we have in common? Sure, we both loved the Lord, but long-term relationships, even for Christians, must have more uniting them than a common eternal destination.

I'll have to say it was pretty cool to be able to tell my friends that I knew the girl who just won a Bronze at the Olympics in Grenoble. My elation was poignantly and a little painfully offset by a weekly reminder of my "unreasonable expectation." Every Saturday the opening sequence on Wide World of Sports featured Janet Lynn landing a perfect double axle into a graceful glide.

Still, the Lord did use me as an instrument in her spiritual life…and for that, I am grateful.

Heavenly Father, I pray that my children will not aim so high as to be inviting failure nor so low as to be ensuring a second-rate success. Amen.

FOR ADDITIONAL READING: ROMANS 12:3; 1CORINTHIANS 3:18-20

THIRTY-TWO

Don We Not Our Gay Apparel

*God made men and women different so
that they might find their complement in each other.
Men attempting to look and act like women or vice versa is
a mockery of God and His design. It only produces confusion, insecurity,
inordinate affection, and emotional instability…all
on the premise of sexual equality.*

It was a long and interesting six months between the time I left for San Diego to prepare a home for your Mother and me and our wedding day in Tulsa. In the first place, it was adventuresome for this Okie to move to California. I arrived in true "Steinbeckian" style, my '65 Chevy Malibu belching blue smoke you could detect for an hour after I passed through each 'berg and 'ville along the way. But I arrived to no *Grapes of Wrath* experience. Rather, I was immediately catapulted into the middle of a ministry making a difference on a global scale: Morris Cerullo World Evangelism (MCWE).

My first place of residence was a little garage apartment on Loring Street in Pacific Beach, just four blocks from the surf. Just a few blocks south of Loring Street was The Action Center, an MCWE ministry outpost right in the middle of the devil's playground. The 24-hour hotline phone number was posted on area billboards and kept weekend phone banks consistently lit up with overdose and counseling calls.

After I was introduced to the small staff and began manning the phones and going on some of the emergency overdose calls, I volunteered to conduct street ministry training classes on Thursday evenings. We usually ended up with ten or twelve faithful young men or women who would go out for a two-hour session in personal witnessing. We didn't have to go far. Across the street to the west was Crystal Pier, under which local addicts would congregate to shoot up, or do "business." Across the street to the south was Maynard's, the southern California Hell's Angels hangout. And directly next door to us (on the east) was Mary's Hang-up, a female impersonator's bar.

I didn't mind going into the Denny's a block away and sitting at the counter on a stool and striking up a conversation with someone, working into the conversation a portion of my testimony. I was a little more intimidated walking down the beach and witnessing to whomever the Lord might direct, but I just couldn't see myself walking in the door at Maynard's or Mary's Hang-up. I usually had my guitar slung over my shoulder when I was on the beach; it seemed to me that it made this Okie appear more Southern Cal. Besides, it was 1973, my hair was over my collar, my "Jesus boots" (sandals) just barely showed beneath my tattered fringe-trimmed bell-bottoms, and I was sporting a disarming ear to ear grin...what was not to like?

Then one evening it happened. I was in the middle of the training part of our street ministry meeting and through our open beachside door staggered a thirty-something gaunt-faced fellow, obviously stoned and clad only in a pair of grungy Bermuda shorts. He weaved his way up to where I was speaking, non-nonchalantly unzipped his fly and proceeded to urinate all over me. Several of the young people in attendance gasped, but I kept on ministering as if nothing were happening. (I know that it might appear that I was being spiritual, silently willing to suffer persecution for the sake of the Lord...but nothing could be farther from the truth. I was simply FREAKED OUT! I chose to ignore it because I didn't have the foggiest idea what an appropriate response would be.)

But it did do something for me. That experience gave me a deep-seated heart of compassion for the lost and a boldness to approach anyone. I reasoned that if there were folks out there that demented, I really needed to "get about my Father's business." Did it embolden me enough to go into one of the adjacent dens of iniquity? It surely did. That evening, after I cleaned up a little, I grabbed my guitar and strode right into Mary's Hang-up. I must have really looked out of place…no skirt, no make-up, no bangles. Still, I unslung my guitar and began to sing loud enough to drown out the jukebox. When I had finished "Amazing Grace" (sung to the tune of "The House of the Rising Sun"), there wasn't a dry eye in the place. For a brief moment you could see their misery through their make-up and their desire for deliverance in their mascara-running eyes. They were captive to their aberration and helpless to do anything about it. Then someone turned up the music so loud that further communication became impossible. I hollered out a prayer for them over the din and walked out.

I have had the opportunity to minister to a variety of sexual miscreants over the years—from transvestites to prostitutes to homosexuals (I just can't use the term "gay" as I've never met the truly *happy* homo). And, although most of them could point to a time in their lives when they weren't that way, they could not find the path back to that time without a great deal of help.

My sons and my daughter, the raiment we don reveals the character we possess. Just as our speech reveals our hearts, our dress reveals our values. It doesn't have to always be fancy or new, but it should always be neat, clean, and appropriate to our station and our gender, and an expression of a modest and pure soul.

God, grant my children the natural sexuality you designed for their genders, with all its attendant strengths and dependencies, that they might find their fulfillment and completion in that person of the opposite sex, which through Your wisdom, they choose. Amen.

For additional reading: John 16:33; Proverbs 11:30

THIRTY-THREE

The Point of No Return

LIES WE'VE BEEN TAUGHT:
You cannot have everything.
(All things are ours, in Christ.)
Ignorance is bliss.
(It isn't; it's hell!)
Might makes right.
(Rather, God makes right. Might makes fright.)
God helps those who help themselves.
(Rather, God helps those who cannot help themselves.)
All good things must come to an end.
(Only God is truly good, and He has no beginning or end.)

When I was the ripe old age of six, I decided I wanted to go visit my favorite Uncle Bill in Texas. Bill was the only brother of my new stepmother, Betty, and he and I had hit it right off. Bill and his wife Dorothy had lived in Muskogee not too far from my new step-grandmother's house when my dad had married Betty two years earlier. Then, his work took him to Texas and I felt abandoned.

Don't tell me where the thought came from, but one day my young mind hatched a plan for going to visit Uncle Bill. I asked my stepmother which way Texas was and she said that it was south of where we lived. Making a bee-line for my closet, I found and donned my new "P.F. Flyers," the tennis-shoe-world's latest high-tech athletic shoes. When she wasn't looking, I took four feathers from her feather duster and sneaked out the garage door. Placing the quill end of the feathers carefully between the knuckles of my fingers, two in each hand, I cautiously approached the runway: the seventy-five-foot long, white, columned front porch of our home. Raring back on my heels as though to get better initial traction, I cut loose all my "engines" and veritably screamed down the rapidly shortening path to…suddenly I had reached the point of no return and was airborne!

My arms had been stiffly arrayed straight out from my sides, the feathers catching the breeze my motion had created. I remember looking over at them approvingly. The moment I left the end of the porch, I elevated the angle of my left arm and lowered the angle of my right arm, fully expecting the desired right-banking climb maneuver to occur. Almost instantly, my stiff aircraft wings became the frantic, flexible wings of a desperate bird on its maiden flight, and I found myself lying dazed on the ground, sputtering grass out my mouth. Fortunately, the altitude at the end of my runway had only been four feet above ground level, and no permanent damage was done. I can still remember the shock of the realization that I really could not fly.

My children, I share this episode of my childhood to underscore the limitations of sincerity and zeal. While one may hold to a belief or a philosophy with all the sincerity of a zealot, the truth of the matter is unaffected by that person's commitment to his or her belief. Indeed, the only result of the most loyal adherence to what turns out to be a lie is a greater disappointment when the truth is finally revealed. And believing some lies can be quite costly.

Lord, grant my children the wisdom to discern the truth and the caution not to embrace a good-sounding lie. Amen.

FOR ADDITIONAL READING: PROVERBS 12:1, 13-15, 17-19, 22

THIRTY-FOUR

Who's Number One?

LIFE'S THREE MOST IMPORTANT DECISIONS:
- *With whom will you spend eternity?*
- *With whom will you spend your life here on earth?*
- *In what endeavor will you expend the measure of your days?*

G etting to "first base" has become a uniquely American idiom. Baseball is our national pastime, and everyone identifies that phrase with arriving at the initial success point of some endeavor ...like pursuing a girl, for instance. A young lady, whom I'll call Barbara, was just one such pursuit of mine.

She and I were both counselors at a camp in eastern Oklahoma during the summer that I transitioned between the Air Force Academy and ORU. We quickly became friends and enjoyed the flighty highs of a summer romance in all of its unrealities. When camp was over and we both went off to our respective collegiate pursuits, we stayed in touch and continued our infatuation in earnest.

Barbara was attending a junior college in the Tulsa area, and it was perhaps too convenient for us to see one another several times each week. I say "too convenient" because our relationship was accelerating toward a slippery slope, toward an intimacy reserved for marriage alone. We had already been more physically involved than I knew God approved of, and I felt a growing conviction that I had passed up first and second base and was rounding third for home!

There was also growing in me an increasing desire for intimacy with God, and the two pursuits were beginning to seem to me more and more at odds. At this same time, doors of ministry were opening up to me and I was beginning to experience the thrill of being used by the Lord in youth evangelism. I am sure Barbara could feel me begin to pull away from her. Her call to me that Friday in late autumn was, I believe now, her desperate attempt to hold on.

"Alan," she said, after we had exchanged the normal pleasantries, "My parents are going to be going out of town for the weekend. Why don't you come on over and spend the weekend with me?" I paused too long, so she added, "We'll have their bedroom all to ourselves."

"Well, Barbara," I began, "You see, uh, well, there's this youth group in Waco I'm supposed to go minister to and…" my voice trailed off.

"Don't you get what I'm saying?" she asked, the frustration in her voice obvious.

"Listen," I dodged, "it's too late to get someone else to take my place. I'm supposed to leave in a couple of hours." She slammed the phone down hard enough for me to jerk the receiver from my ear in self-defense.

Monday after the weekend, there was no call. By Tuesday, the unresolved conflict in my heart was screaming for resolution…so I called her. "Barbara, we need to talk." We agreed to get together that evening for one of those defining-moment conversations that are so essential in every relationship. When she got in my car, I blurted out, "Barbara, who is number one in your life?"

"Why, you are," she replied quite matter-of-factly.

"Okay. Now ask me the same question," I said.

"What? Okay, who is number one in your life?"

"Well, it isn't you, Barbara," I replied. "You're number two."

"You mean, there's someone else?" she asked, her voice rising. "Is it another woman?"

"Yes, there is someone else, but He's a man," I said.

"A man?!" she exclaimed.

"Hold on," I said quickly. "Let me explain."

"Barbara, I cannot continue in this relationship. It is completely unfair to you. I am number one in your life, but Jesus is number one in mine. The best you can ever hope for is number two."

The rest of the conversation is a blur to me. I'm sure she cried…I probably did, too. We both had a lot invested emotionally in the relationship, but it could never prosper and I knew it. Barbara was a great girl, but our relationship was two dimensional. There was no spiritual component…nor could there have been because of our lust for one another.

I learned a couple of valuable lessons in the pain I experienced (and that I inflicted). First, going too far before God's timing eliminates the possibilities of God's blessing on a relationship. Second, having our priorities right makes decisions in life, especially the difficult ones, much easier. I did finally meet a young lady who could only place me at the number two spot as well…and I'm happily spending the rest of my life with her.

Lord Jesus, thank you that all of my children have made the first decision first and correctly. Now, grant that they find that spouse whose complementary gifts supply the needed remainder for their appointed destiny. Amen.

FOR ADDITIONAL READING: ECCLESIASTES 3:1-8; MATTHEW 6:33

THIRTY-FIVE

A Song of Worth

It is a true statement that, in ourselves,
none of us are worthy.
But it is also true that none of us are worthless.
Indeed, if something is worth whatever the buyer is willing to pay for it,
then each of you,
my children, are valuable beyond measure, for you were bought with the
inestimable price of the blood of God's own Son.

One of the heroes in my life is an amazing woman named Hettie Lou Brooks. You, my children, are blessed to have known her as well. You remember that I was a counselor at her Brookhill Ranch Summer Camp (1972-1973), but you probably didn't know that neither she nor her son, Tim Brooks, would ever accept a penny for all the weeks of camps you went through over the years. They saw it as an investment in your future, which is the reason they founded the camp in the first place.

Hettie's unusual sense of value is reflected in the life of selfless service she has lived throughout the years I have known her. Her famous "story time" at camp has captivated literally tens of thousands of young people over the years. Her efforts on the mission field in Belize, Central America, have changed the lives of a generation of youth there. The thousands and thousands of women whose lives have been forever changed by the Christian principles she has taught in her seminars have taken their transformations home to their families and multiplied her ministry. And to this quite partial list of her accomplishments, I have to add the difference she has made in my life.

One example of that difference is the life lesson I learned one Sunday morning just weeks after Hettie had founded Christian Ministries Church. She had, as usual, preached a powerful message, but I had already endured enough July heat in the open-air camp pavilion that I was more than a little ready for the end of the service. That is when Hettie asked a lady I did not know to close the service with a song.

She stood and smiled, then opened her mouth and out came the most horrifying excuse for a song I have ever heard…and acapella at that! When she finished the verse, she began the chorus, a little louder and even screechier than before. Dear Jesus, I thought, Hettie must be mortified. Here she is trying to start a church and all these new folks here will surely think twice before coming back next week. I guess she didn't know that this woman sounded worse than a barnyard of guineas. But when I glanced over at Hettie it was no painful grimace I saw. To my incredulous amazement, Hettie had her eyes closed and the most peaceful, enraptured expression on her face I had ever seen.

This woman must be completely tone deaf! How could Hettie allow this to continue, let alone appear to be enjoying it? I was mystified. Then, as suddenly as the aural havoc had begun, it stopped. Sweet relief! I nearly gasped at the contrast…what peaceful tranquility. But to my astonishment, she began a second and later a third verse, each punctuated by an increased volume at the chorus. Lord, have mercy, I thought; when is the agony going to end?

Finally, at the end of the third ear-splitting rendering of the chorus, she stopped. Then Hettie dreamily opened her eyes and said, "That was so heavenly, Sister. Thank you for using your gift to bless us. Please, could you sing us just one more verse?"

I wanted to bolt from the building or at least cover my ears. I looked at others in the audience and they were also exchanging glances amongst themselves. What was Hettie thinking of…and there it was again, that look of complete and utter joy spread across her face.

When that annoying event was over and people were just milling about fellowshipping with one another, I honestly felt like going up to some of the ones I had seen cringing and making excuses for Hettie. I wanted to tell them that this was not our usual service…or that Hettie had forgotten to change the battery in her hearing aid…or something!

I must have had a dazed and pained expression of helplessness on my face because Hettie came up to me and asked me what I thought of the beautiful solo at the end of the service. "Well, I…I…I don't think I've ever heard anything quite like that," I managed at last. "Why in the world did you ask for more?"

Hettie's reply was classic. "Did you see the expression on her face? I saw the one on yours. She obviously needed to sing that song a lot more than you thought you needed to hear it." I felt about an inch tall at that moment and wondered if I could ever attain to the depth of understanding and maturity I had just seen in Hettie.

My children, worth and value are a lot more internal than external. Man looks on the outward appearance, but God looks at the heart. Adopting God's value system begins by seeing yourself and others as He does.

Father, give my children the revelation of their worth in Your eyes and let their esteem for others grow out of the knowledge that for each, You paid no less. Amen.

For additional reading: Romans 12:16; Philippians 2:3

THIRTY-SIX

Givers and Takers

A hard worker is always asking what he can do next.

Tom Erwin, a friend of mine that all of you children have known most of your lives, sings a song with the line, "There are only two kinds of people, only two lives that we can live, those who take and those who give." [7] I have always liked that song because it so clearly separates the world into two camps—givers and takers ... and I have certainly known both.

Your grandfather Sargent was certainly a giver. He was generous to people who were in need almost to a fault, but he did believe in "workfare," rather than welfare. He believed that giving to someone sometimes meant putting a shovel in an outstretched hand rather than giving a handout. Even the allowances he "gave" your Uncle Mark and me were on the condition of a completed chores list.

No doubt his influence in my life was the inspiration for the way I dealt with the following situation. One day I was driving to the local Wally-World to pick up something and happened to pull up to a stoplight where a well-weathered middle-aged man in Salvation Army hand-me-downs was holding out a sign: *Will Work for Food*. I met his eye and then drove slowly on past as an idea began to germinate…I wondered if he really wanted work, or was he counting on people to be sympathetic and throw him a couple of dollars?

I pulled into the store, went straight to the school supply section and got what I needed. Once back at my truck, I printed with a large black marker on my poster-board: *Will Feed for Work.* Driving back around to the intersection with my new sign taped to the side of my truck, which would be opposite his position on the street corner, I pulled alongside, honked to get his attention and then pointed to the sign on my truck. He had a funny expression on his face for a moment, then he shook his head and waved me on.

My children, if "idle hands are the devil's workshop" then willing hands are the Lord's. Work is not part of "the Curse," for Adam and Eve had a job before their fall from grace. They were instructed to tend and keep the garden and to subdue it. Labor became more toilsome after God put a curse on the ground, as He said it would no longer yield its fruit willingly. God's creation was not going to cooperate with a man who was in rebellion against the Creator.

My encouragement to you here is to show yourself faithful...to the task at hand, to the employer who is entrusting you with the management of his resources, to the Lord who expects you to do everything "as unto Him." A giver is someone who sees what needs to be done and does it without wondering if the man who labors alongside him is doing his share. A good worker is someone who is anticipating the need of his boss and getting the job done without having to be told every little detail of what is expected of him. The diligent man is always looking for what needs to be done next, not for a place to stand where he might be overlooked.

As diligence is the fruit of patience, Lord, so grant my children those experiences which bear fruit in a Godly character. Amen

For additional reading: Proverbs 6:10-11; 2 Thessalonians 3:10-12

THIRTY-SEVEN

Catalytic Converters

My son, there are few things that distress a father more
than strife between brothers.
This is at least as true with your Heavenly Father.
And there is nothing that distresses children more than
strife between parents.

I f you were to ask me if I had had a happy childhood, I would immediately reply: yes! I am sure there are those who would similarly
respond who are in delusion, others who are in denial, and still others
who have selective memories…and even many who, from anyone's perspective, did indeed, have happy childhoods. However, I am inclined to
believe that the majority of those who would respond with me in the affir-
mative are, like me, simply optimistic. In spite of the occasional emotional
upheaval and the generic trauma associated with growing up, I view my
early life as a definitely positive and hugely rewarding experience.

This is not to say that all who have shared similar circumstances
would reach similar conclusions. There are many of life's difficulties that
are designed to be character catalysts. They always produce change.
Whether they turn out to be positive or negative, constructive or destructive, is often a matter of attitude. The following will serve as an example
of my point.

The summer before my first grade year, my dad and his contractor
brother-in-law built a house on a choice lot in a new subdivision that Dad
had just finished surveying. Built in the progressive 1950's, it was designed
with some of the latest technological advances available…like central heat
and wall-to-wall carpeting! Since my older brother and I were pretty hard

on the carpeting, it was soon removed and we were back down to hardwood flooring. Mysteriously, that's about the same time that strife entered our home.

At first, my dad and my first stepmother didn't bicker in public, but they unloaded all their repressed frustrations after they shut their bedroom door at night. I could hear every word as it echoed through the ductwork, and I found sleep, when it came, a welcome relief. It was sometime between those first "broadcasts" and the escalating strife that became open warfare that my growing determination congealed into concrete purpose. Never, I promised, would I allow conflict to become a way of life in my home. Never, ever would I speak those unretractable and destructive terms like "divorce" or "I hate you."

Your mother and I have definitely had our differences, but we have never allowed them to mature into strife! While they were yet mere disagreements, we reflected upon the disastrous consequences that strife had borne out in other families and concluded that we preferred peace to always having to be right.

Prince of Peace, may my children come to the realization that peace is not the absence of conflict but the presence of your Holy Spirit. Amen.

FOR ADDITIONAL READING: PSALM 34:14; HEBREWS 12:14-15

THIRTY-EIGHT

Having the Time of My Life

If a chair could have emotions,
it would find its greatest fulfillment in being sat upon.
If you will consider your life His throne, then you will come to enjoy
the complete contentment that is the portion of each creature who
does that for which they were created.

Sometime during the final week of my senior year at Muskogee High School, my physics teacher, Mr. Jeffries, pulled me aside for a few words. He had been my favorite instructor and I felt we had a pretty good rapport, so that is why I was taken aback by his words. "Alan," he said, "If you ever want to make something of yourself, you're going to have to give yourself to just one thing. Your interests are too varied. You must focus. To be the best at anything, it has to be the only thing."

I thanked him for his input, of course, but I pondered on his words for a long time. *What was his beef, I thought? I had made an "A" in his class. What did he want, anyway?* Then I remembered the little rhyme my first grade teacher, Mrs. Crowder, had taught us: "One at a time, and that done well, is a very good rule, as many can tell."

Okay, kids…you know me. Those were great admonitions, but I obviously never took the advice either of them gave. My whole life has been ten simultaneous involvements after another. As much as I would like to justify the hyperactive nature of my pursuits in life, I must confess that I have arrived at the "Jack-of-all-trades, master-of-none" destination. The only consolation I have is that I have loved every minute of it!

So, I'm not really very good at anything…no real cause for boasting … and I can live with that. Then again, there is this one thing that I love to do more than anything. I love to teach. As I look back on the most ful-filling moments of my life, I realize they inevitably involved helping to steer the course of some student or another. When I was fourteen and on counselor staff at Boy Scout Camp, I was trying to teach younger scouts how to tie knots. Today, as Dean of Students at Applied Life Christian College, I find myself spending a lot of time teaching students how to untie the knots their unwise decisions have created.

I was made for teaching. Do you know how I know that for sure? Because that is when I feel the anointing of God flowing freely through me, because it never drains me—it always energizes me. I cannot help myself...thirty seconds into a casual conversation with anyone not my peer, and I find myself attempting to communicate some deep truth about something. I'm sure it's quite obnoxious, at times.

My point here, children, is how to be happy in life. Find out what it is that you were created to do and do it. Only then will you find the hap-piness that comes from fulfilling the will of God for your life. What is it that you *love* to do? What is it that *energizes* you? What pursuit is *compul-sive* for you? What is it that you are *doing* when you feel the anointing of God flowing through you? *That* is what you were created to do.

I guess my teachers were right after all. There really is just one area on which I focus...I teach. Interestingly enough, all the various interests I have had over the years have made it possible to increase the breadth of my relevance to the students I teach...and I am having the time of my life.

Dear Lord, be Lord. Amen.

For additional reading: 2 Corinthians 12:9; Romans 12:2

THIRTY-NINE

My Comet Experience

You can never say, "No, Lord." If you say, "No," then He is not Lord.

Submission may be the most difficult assignment any young woman faces. Although I think it is easier for a wife to submit to her husband if she has learned submission to her father in the home, I still think for you to consciously sacrifice your own agenda to adopt the agenda of someone else is not easy. The same is at least as true for men in regard to their submission to the Lord.

Your mother has been the finest example of submission I have ever known. She might disagree with my assessment, but that is because she is much too humble ever to take credit for the unseen supporting role she has consistently played in our marriage. You see, she has come to the place in her relationship with me that she sees her submission as a "sub" *mission*. Lynn has never sought the limelight but always rejoiced in my victories without seeking any recognition for the vital role she has played in each of them. And, when I suffered a defeat, she has always tried to lay the bulk of the failure at her own feet… She would usually have uttered, "If only I had prayed harder" (or some such self-deprecating remark).

True submission is more than just grudging obedience. It involves more than a temporary accommodation to someone else's ideas, plans and methods. Rather, true submission involves an irrevocable commitment to the success of another, even delighting to be asked to have whatever small part might be asked of you. I wish I could say I have faithfully demonstrated that same level of submission to the Lord's purposes and plans.

I shall never forget the night I finally and fully submitted to the Lord's will for my life. I was sitting in a red 1962 Comet that my friend and mentor, Guy Ames, owned. We were parked off the highway a bit at a road construction site somewhere in south Tulsa. I was on Spring Break from the Air Force Academy and had decided to visit Guy and perhaps get some guidance. About a month earlier, I had written him concerning my confusion at being at the Academy, the call I felt I had on my life and the contradiction my present course seemed to present. Guy and I had gone to a new Easter cantata that ORU student Dave Stearman had just written, *God Come Down,* and afterward Guy invited me to dinner. After the meal, he looked at me and said, "Well, are you ready?"

"Ready for what?" I asked.

"To be filled with the Holy Spirit," he said quite matter-of-factly. Without waiting for my response, he rose and paid the check. Sitting in the dark in his car fifteen minutes later, I could sense the destiny of the moment. I had asked Jesus to forgive me of my sins and had surrendered to Him as my Savior just over a year earlier. Still, I knew that something was missing.

Then Guy explained how the disciples had been instructed to go into all the world but had been told to "tarry ye in Jerusalem until ye be endued with power from on high" (Luke 24:49). Guy said that the "something missing" I needed was the power of the Holy Spirit. He said that the Holy Spirit would make it clear to me what I should be doing with my life when I submitted completely to the Lordship of Christ. I wasn't sure at that point just what he was talking about, but somehow I knew if he would pray for me I would get the peace and direction I was seeking.

I was correct. Although I didn't understand then all of what would later occur as a result of that prayer, I did get the peace and direction I needed. I decided right then and there to live the rest of my life for the Lord—to surrender to whatever calling He would have for me…except, of course, to go into the ministry. That would be just a little "over the edge." I would be faithful to attend church, to read my Bible, to pray as the need arose...no problem...*but not full time ministry*...surely He would not expect *that*.

Never say never. The whole concept of Lordship is that you have given up your agenda for His. It would be oxymoronic to say, "No, Lord." If He is not Lord *of* all, He is not Lord *at* all.

As you children all now know, I have been in the ministry ever since. In fact, I have come to the understanding of the universality of God's calling—*Every Christian a minister.* I cannot adequately express the richness of experience that serving God unconditionally has been to me or the magnitude of the joy it has given me. This fulfillment is a direct result of the realization that my submission to God is a *sub*-mission—I am a vital part of God's work in the earth.

May Your Lordship be the highest aim of my children, and obeying You their primary objective. Amen.

For additional reading: Mark 14:36; Matthew 7:21

FORTY

Farewell to Cindy

When is a child old enough to drive a car?
The answer is at whatever time after the legal age that he or she
has come to respect the law, human life, and the potential to kill that
resides in 2,000 pounds of steel and glass!

To be in a place so different, so foreign,
Required a grace and strength not mine,
So recently changed, my new heart abhorring
The Cadre's expressions of moral decline.

The Lord heard my plea, for sin can so test you,
He sent me an angel to take me away.
Her father a colonel, an unlikely rescue,
They invited me home for dinner one day.

I had signed up for chapel corps and choir,
Took every chance to escape that I could.
The only serenity I grew to require
Was galloping with Cindy in the five-acre wood.

She was too young to be but a fancy,
So sweet and so pretty, her parent's delight,
Had the time and place differed, there was a chance we
Might have waited until the timing was right.

I then turned a corner in the journey of life,
Surrendered my own dreams to wholly seek God.
Three years would pass till I found a wife,
Together no sorrow our new journey trod.

I'd not forgotten that angel so youthful,
Sent me when I was so awfully alone.
Shared in a letter my joy in betrothal,
But heard nothing back by letter or phone.

When Lynn and I settled into our first home,
And our first day's mail had arrived,
We sadly read a Mom's tragic tome
Of how her sweet angel had died.

It seems that Cindy and five of her friends
Had careened down a dark road too fast;
A terrified cat, a screeching brake sends
Six girls full of hope to their last.

I wept for her Dad, for her Mom and her Sister,
For Corky, her brother who'd loved her so much;
I prayed for all I knew who would miss her,
And promised I'd stay in close touch.

It proved too painful to continue to write,
I needed the memory to dim,
Till now I've not dredged up that terrible sight,
But at last I can see things less grim.

If sharing my feelings in all of their sadness
Can cause my own children to learn,
Then sorrow finds purpose and I find gladness,
From tragedy fools' lessons discern.

Lord Jesus, give my children the ability to see an accident coming long before it happens, the quickness of reflex to avert disaster, and the soberness of mind that usually comes only long after the tragedy occurs…and let this prayer apply to all areas of their lives. Amen.

FOR ADDITIONAL READING: PROVERBS 15:31-32; 22:3, 27:12

FORTY-ONE

Being Puzzled

My children, I have a puzzle and a box. The puzzle is titled "My Understanding of Things" and my box is labeled "Things to Be Resolved Later." The puzzle started out quite small but grew larger every time I added a piece from my collection in the box. And the box, while not emptying from my labors, also became larger and fuller with the removal and placement of each piece. The pursuit of understanding is, after all, the pursuit of God.

My children, there are four ways you can learn anything:

1. BY OBSERVATION (this occurs when you receive input by way of your five senses and draw conclusions from the comparisons you make with those things you already know);

2. BY RELATION (this occurs as you listen or read someone relating what they have learned and accept their account as fact);

3. BY EXPERIENCE (this occurs when you learn something empirically, actually living out the lesson as it is being taught);

4. BY REVELATION (this occurs on a spirit to spirit level; you receive knowledge in whole form not having to have the benefit of observation, relation or experience; you know what has been revealed to your spirit and your mind accepts it without demanding corroboration).

Many will argue about the validity of the fourth means...those for whom this method of learning is outside their experience...those who might argue that God does not exist or that if He does, He would not deign to communicate to so insignificant a creature as man. But revelation can only be spiritually discerned, and those who have not had their "still-born" spirits regenerated by the Holy Spirit cannot receive this kind of knowledge.

I only share this with you to relieve what frustration you may experience from time to time as you seek the truth in life. You see, God reveals Himself to man on a "need-to-know" basis. We usually think we need to know, but God, Who sees the end from the beginning, also sees what a mess we'll make of things as we try to help Him effect His purposes. As the old saying goes, "A little knowledge is dangerous;"[7] and that is all we, in our little finite minds, can ever really have...a little knowledge.

Rather, we should trust the Lord. In fact, the Lord is constantly putting us in situations with insufficient information so that we have to trust Him. It is by the exercise of this trust or faith that our souls mature. The puzzle will never be finished, and that is good news. Who wants to serve a God who is entirely within our grasp? My God is too great to completely know, too deep for His depth to ever be plumbed, too wonderful for me to ever stop wondering!

Great and Mighty God, though my children may not ever fully apprehend You, may they ever pursue You. In their frustration at their lack of understanding, may they find the comfort of your revelation and the faith for their convictions. Amen.

FOR ADDITIONAL READING: PSALM 139:7-11; EPHESIANS 3:20

FORTY-TWO

Above the Fray

*We struggle in vain to guard against those things which
attack from without when we make no attempt to repel those things which
attack from within.*

Full of gratitude for so much love,
Sent by God on the wings of a dove.
The Spirit that fills me, the Presence that thrills me,
A God that wills me to live above.

Above the attitude my weakness spawns,
I find God's strength through my darkness dawns.
Each hopeful ray soon lights my way,
And bids me stay the demon pawns.

The strength within I've come to find
Is God's own grace to rule my mind.
The enemy flees when soon he sees
Temptation's pleas I now can bind.

The power of sin cannot hold sway
God's Word in my mouth will rule the day.
The authority I use unmasks the ruse
Sent to confuse and make me pay.

Pay for that which Jesus has bought,
The freedom all men have ever sought;
But we should trust as sons of dust,
And live we must as we know we ought,
Ever above the fray.

Father, may my children have the mind of Christ, the courage He demonstrated at the cross, and the wisdom to know that "with us is the Lord our God to help us, and to fight our battles" (2 Chronicles 32:8.) Amen.

FOR ADDITIONAL READING: EPHESIANS 6:12-18; 1 CORINTHIANS 2:16; PHILIPPIANS 2:5

FORTY-THREE

Busted

Many in their efforts to "be cool" have become lukewarm.

(SEE REVELATIONS 3:16)

The need for acceptance and approval is one of the most powerful drives in the human psyche. This drive may even find its root on the instinctive level, like the instinct for survival. I believe that it is so powerful because, like our drive to survive, it was placed there by God—the acceptance and approval of the creature by its Creator. The difficulty comes when this drive for acceptance gets misappropriated. Intended by God to steer us down a moral path of behavior toward a life pleasing to Him, we rather look for the acceptance and approval of our peers. Wise parents, acknowledging that this misappropriation is quite inevitable in their immature children, will carefully guide their choices of friends and acquaintances.

For a teenager, this drive for acceptance is also part of the young person's pursuit of his or her individual identity. Looking back on some of the ridiculous things I did in my own "stupid phase," I can only explain them by attributing my actions to this drive.

I remember going to Lake Fort Gibson one day (I think it was senior skip day), for several of my classmates had secured a ski boat and an ice chest full of beer. For a nerd like me to be invited to spend the day with them was like winning the lottery. Did I want to go, they asked? You bet, I responded, without hesitation.

Although I hated (and always have) the taste of beer, I put the open can to my lips and pretended to glug down its contents, while actually pouring it over the side of the boat when my buds (no pun intended) were not looking. I wanted them to think of me as "one of the guys" and not a "square." This ruse did produce the desired result, as my popularity with this crowd soared. I began to get invited to other outings and, although I fended off most of their entreaties with plausible excuses, I went to some and left before things got out of hand. I didn't agree with their values but I wanted their acceptance. I even justified my actions by reasoning that I would be influencing them as well, and for the good.

The reality of running with the wrong crowd is that you end up going where they go and getting what they (and always to your surprise) and you deserve. Compromise always ultimately results in disappointment… in those in whom you have trusted and in yourself.

It seemed like a good idea at the time (one of those "famous last words"). We were going to spend the night on the access road in front of Muskogee High School on the eve of our senior picnic so that we could be first in line in the caravan to the lake. By "we" I mean Mac Harris and I and a few of our contemporaries. Mac had driven his folks old Mercedes, and we had brought sleeping bags which we laid out next to the car on the still-warm asphalt. Mac had a fifth of some alcoholic beverage which I am sure he probably "borrowed" from his parents' liquor cabinet.

I had only done my usual bottle to the lips routine and we hadn't been there long enough for Mac to be soused. Suddenly, the police were there. Their siren squawked and blue lights flashed…and then we were blinded by the glare of powerful flashlights shone directly into our eyes from close range. Busted! The open bottle they found in the car was sufficient for them, and we were headed in the squad car for jail!

I shall *never* forget the booking process…emptying our pockets, getting fingerprinted, the rough manner in which we were spoken to…the humiliation and the fear. What was my dad going to say? And what was this going to do to our chances at a service academy appointment? Mac had received an appointment to West Point and I had pursued the Air Force Academy where Mac's brother, Jim, was already attending.

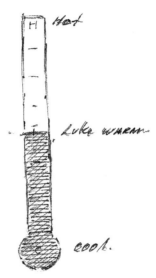

They put us in the Juvenile Women's holding cell and Mac and I lamented our fate together. At 4:00 A.M. the duty officer came to retrieve us and released us into the custody of Mac's father. They had decided not to press charges, we were told, and we each breathed a huge sigh of relief, followed, of course, by a lengthy discourse on the folly of our ways by Mr. Harris. I don't remember anything he said, being completely worn out by the ordeal, hoping that my dad would not find out and thinking how completely stupid our actions had been.

It was not until twenty years later that I learned that my dad and Mr. Harris had set us up. Knowing that Mac had taken the alcohol, they contacted a friend on the local police force and arranged the whole thing. It was a lesson that was not lost on either of us! It produced in me the necessary circumspectness to retrieve me from the brink of what only could have been an increasing number of progressively more foolish compromises of my integrity.

I have processed mentally the events of that "stupid phase" in my life many times over the years and have come to the conclusion that acceptance and approval are only as good for you as the ones from whom it is received. God's acceptance I already have because of what Jesus did for me on the cross, and His approval always comes when I have demonstrated my gratitude for His acceptance by living a life worthy of the gift.

Lord of love, show my children their true worth by revealing to them the price you have paid for them and let them labor for your approval successfully by finding and following the path of your perfect will. Amen.

FOR ADDITIONAL READING: 1 CORINTHIANS 5:11; 15:33

FORTY-FOUR

Measuring Up

If "who you are" is measured in terms of "what you do," then
who will you be when you are no longer doing what you were doing?
Herein lies the source of all identity crises.
Who you are should be measured in terms of your value to God
rather than your value to men.

Perhaps it is a sign of the times, but the incidence rate for what psychologists term "mid-life crises" is epidemic. Everyone knows someone who is having doubts about himself...he has lost his job due to downsizing, or is a casualty of an economic downturn, or is just feeling that life is passing him by. Having arrived at middle age, the temporality of his existence suddenly dawns upon him, and he looks back on his past with regret and on his future with uncertainty. This is when the symptoms of a mid-life crisis begin to appear. He thinks an affair will bring him back the zest his boring marriage has failed to deliver or reassure him that he is still attractive and virile.

Men are not the only ones subject to this malady. Women who have empty nests often feel this same sense of bewilderment...lost and confused about their self-worth and filled with depression.

Both men and women who are suffering in this condition are really suffering from a relationship vacuum...and I am not talking about their relationships with their spouses. I am talking about their relationships with God. You see, my sons and my daughter, all human relations spring from and are a reflection of our relationship with God. Man has a vertical relationship with God upon which all the horizontal relationships with man rest. If the vertical relationship is secure, then the horizontal relationships prosper.

Jesus put it this way when the Pharisees tried to trip Him up with a question about the greatest commandment. He answered: "Thou shalt love the Lord thy God with all thy heart, and with all thy soul, and with all thy mind…and thou shalt love thy neighbor as thyself" (see Matthew 22:34-40). When our relationship with God is right, it only follows that our relationships with mankind will also be right. This is why I think that the cross, with its vertical and horizontal timbers, is such an appropriate icon for Christianity. Christ Himself is that vertical timber connecting God with man for the first time since Adam sinned, and His outstretched arms pinned to the horizontal timber express His loving example to the very world that rejected Him.

When your mother and I lived in San Diego during the first few years of our marriage, I had the opportunity of attending a Catholic Charismatic seminar on the ministry of the Holy Spirit. One of the workshops I attended was led by the pastor of a medium-sized Baptist church in Chula Vista. What made this church unique was not its ministry *in* the community, but rather its ministry *by* community. This church had felt a call to community living.

Apparently, all of their members lived in one of about a dozen homes, each housing twenty or more parishioners, often representing three or four families per dwelling. *Some* would hold down jobs in the nearby town, bringing in an income for the support of the household; *some* would remain at home during the day, taking care of the responsibilities of housekeeping, laundry and cooking; still *others* were freed to what they termed "twenty-four-hour ministry." The objects of their intensive ministry efforts were individuals in need of a complete overhaul, so to speak—drug-dependent youths wanting to find a way out of their addictions, unmarried pregnant teens who had decided not to terminate their pregnancies but had been rejected by their families, and men and women who were suffering from the disorientation of mid-life crises.

One such recipient of this intensive and individual ministry was a retired naval captain. While in the service, he had commanded an aircraft carrier with more than a thousand men on board. As his post-military retirement had begun, so had the debilitating depression in which he found himself. Having been referred by a counselor to Pastor Ken Haggard's community church, he soon found his crisis beginning to unravel.

The pastor explained to us at the workshop that their house rules were such that new additions to the "family" were not allowed to do anything for themselves. They could not serve themselves at the table, could not make their own beds, and could not even help with the dishes or do anything else. The purpose, the pastor said, was to help each individual to whom they were ministering find out who he or she really was. Everyone, he said, thinks of himself in terms of what he does. The Captain saw himself as a leader of a thousand men, the commander of a multi-billion dollar vessel. When in retirement those defining accoutrements had been removed, the ensuing identity crisis was the result. By not allowing the retired captain to lift a finger the first month of his stay in his new home, the pastor was stripping his identity down to its core meaning. "Who am I?" could no longer be tied to what he did.

And that is why their ministry to men such as the captain was so effective. As Christians, who we are is a direct result of who our Father is. When all else has been stripped away, each of us is still a child of God, and that fact becomes our anchor. The security of our relationship with God becomes the source of our unshakable sense of destiny and purpose. The "Why am I here?" question that usually follows the first question is actually answered by it. As a child of God, I am here to do the works of God. All the "doing" in my life might change from time to time, but I am not defined by that anyway. My identity is in Who it is that birthed me, and the what He birthed me for is the expression of that identity, not the other way around.

Our worth is not measured by what we do, but by Whose we are.

Lord Jesus, as you have come to destroy the works of the devil, may I follow in your footsteps. As you have come to bring life and life more abundantly, may I do the same. As my children are also yours, may my example never confuse them as to my or their true identities or worth. Amen.

FOR ADDITIONAL READING: JOHN 10:10; 17:18

FORTY-FIVE

Saints' Redemption

Lust demands, "What can I get?" … Love asks, "What can I give?"

"Thou shalt not!" and arched walls echoed
The commandments' edicts faint,
Then the preacher spotted the rapt sweet face
Of precious Sarah Saint.

She hadn't been coming for such a long time,
He thought he'd dodged his deed,
That one dark night, his counsel sought,
He'd sown that one wild seed.

It had scared him greatly to see face on
The lust that lurked within;
But single and strong he'd thought himself,
'Twas pride that brought him sin.

As he'd wrestled that night and sought the Lord
To free him from his guilt,
Forgiveness came and with it peace,
No thought for consequences built.

The altar call given for "those who'd come
With a broken and contrite heart,"
She stood to her feet, squeezed to the aisle,
And gave that preacher a start!

For there revealed in full-term glory
Was the product of his weakness,
Self-righteous pride now chased away,
Replaced by tearful meekness.

First he was to hit his knees,
Being right there at the altar,
He didn't care what others thought,
His repentance must not falter.

Kneeling beside, she took his hand
And whispered in his ear,
"It's not yours, I'm sorry to say,
There's nothing for you to fear."

There had been so many, she then explained,
With precautions she'd failed to bother;
Repentant late, her child now due,
Would arrive without a father.

He squeezed her arm and slowly smiled,
Then raising her to her feet,
He knelt again and took her hand,
In sacrifice so sweet.

"Ladies and gentlemen, meet my wife,
If she'll have me, I mean to say;

For what the devil meant to destroy
Is redeemed for us today."

God can turn any disaster
Into perfection to be admired;
A repentant heart, a submitted will,
Is all that is required.

Most Merciful God, Who in Your relentless desire to bless me has so often and so completely washed away the stain of my sin, grant that my children will learn that the currency of love is sacrifice and the currency of lust is selfishness. May they accumulate to their account the former without ever experiencing the bitter enslavement of the latter. Amen.

FOR ADDITIONAL READING: JOHN 8:11; 1 JOHN 1:9

FORTY-SIX

Unintended Consequences

A word spoken is like a stone thrown, once relased it cannot be recalled.

I suppose that one of the earliest symptoms of terminal boyhood is throwing rocks. When my dad would take my brother and me fishing, I would get so excited at the prospects of catching "the big one"—you know, the one that my dad always said "got away." But if I didn't catch anything in the first five minutes, the smooth oval stones of the river bank quickly became too great a temptation, and I soon became engrossed in trying to get them all back in the water. It wasn't that my five-year old immaturity evidenced itself in a short attention span, for I could throw rocks for hours. I was fascinated by the infinite variations of color, size and shape of the stones as well as by the different sounds they made as they entered the water at varying angles.

No one can relate to this unless they've been subject to this same addiction. The whir of an oblong sharp-sided rock as it is being spun off the fingertips of a young boy produces a lingering smile. The destruction of stick and paper bridges carefully constructed over the gaping chasms of puddle-sized lakes accompanied by the orally produced sound effects of falling bombs makes for untold hours of lazy summer afternoon rock-throwing entertainment.

There were a few occasions, however, when this blissful activity was interrupted by the painful consequence inherent in the hazardous habit.

One summer my grandparents on my mother's side, the Israel's, took my brother and me for a three-and-half-week summer adventure traveling up through the Appalachians and the Alleghenies to New York. We finally stopped in York Beach, Maine, for a week-long stay in a quaint cottage on Nubble Lighthouse's peninsula. At ten years of age I had graduated from the childish primitiveness of a hand-hurled rock to all manner of sophisticated catapulting systems, and I soon discovered the incredible rock-lobbing properties of the tough wide bands of seaweed that covered the rock outcroppings of the point. I sent every loose stone I could find plunging into the approaching breakers fifty or more yards into the Atlantic.

My brother, who was not the avid hurler I was, wandered off down the shore exploring every nook and cranny, searching for starfish to add to our growing fetid collection. I knew where he was more or less, although I only saw his head bob up and down amongst the boulders. Who knows why a boy gets the stupid lame brain notions that come into his head. For some reason the thought, "I wonder how close to my brother I could chunk one of these stones," presented itself in mischievous fashion in my mind. Before reason could assault impetuousness, I let the stone fly from my weed-sling and watched with fascinated dread its fated trajectory. My hollered warning was lost in the sound of the surf but both were shattered by the scream of pain my brother let out as the rock found its mark.

My brother clambered bloody and screaming over the rocks toward the cottage and the comforting arms of my grandmother. I made my way hurriedly too, in the opposite direction. When I finally came in an hour later, no amount of excuses given or remorse demonstrated seemed to have any effect. "You could have put his eye out," my Grandmother exclaimed! And the two-inch scar over his right eye attests to this day the unretractable nature of my foolishness.

Many times since then I have recalled that incident and experienced the same helplessness I felt as I regretted some foolish remark thoughtlessly hurled at someone. How I have wished to alter its course or change its impact, but to no avail. That, my children, is what discretion is all about.

Living Lord, help me teach my children the power of word and deed, that they might sow in wisdom and not reap in unintended consequences. May they learn to think before they act and listen before they speak. Amen.

FOR ADDITIONAL READING: JAMES 3:1-13; LUKE 14:28-32

FORTY-SEVEN

Truth's Vista

Lack of understanding is often a product of perspective.
That is why the coach sends in the plays from the sidelines.
His understanding has been increased by his higher perspective.
When we don't understand why our lives have taken their present courses,
it is simply because we don't have the higher perspective of God.
But it is possible to trust without understanding. That is what faith is.

Too close the forest to see the trees?
Life's best viewed upon one's knees
For Providence revealed.
Much that's seen to be confusing
Gives rise to theories' endless musing
And further truths concealed.

To rise above the common thought
And see what others only sought
But never apprehended,
Provides perspective, makes one wise,
Helps remove Deception's guise
As truth is comprehended.

How to make this sage ascent,
Acquire the vista heaven sent,
To know what none can guess?
Just open the Book, incline the ear,
Listen with faith, dismiss the fear,
And learn the Truth, no less.

Lord of Light, reveal to my children the truth of every circumstance by elevating their perspective to Yours. May they be discerning, yet discreet; knowledgeable, yet humble; decisive though patient. Amen.

FOR ADDITIONAL READING: ISAIAH 55:8-9; REVELATION 22:13

FORTY-EIGHT

Commit

To not decide is to decide. Neutrality is a myth.

When faced with naught but turning tides
And wayward strides,
Chaos confides
Is slippery slides,
Commit.

If met with choice of chance or fate
Or pressed to wait,
Act now, be late,
Don't hesitate,
Commit.

This orb be full of he who stands
Between two hands
While time like sands
Falls 'tween the bands,

Of weakened will,
I've had my fill,
Yet speak I still,
Ascend the hill,
Commit.

God, our Sovereign, who knows no separation between to will and to do, may you impart that same resolve to my children that you displayed in Gethsemane; and may they pray with you, "not my will, but Thine, be done." (Luke 22:42). Amen.

FOR ADDITIONAL READING: JAMES 1:5-8; PROVERBS 16:3

FORTY-NINE

The Color of Love

True love is not "love because of" but rather "love in spite of."

Black as night, the ugly sight
Our sin-wrought visage bore
Chased away all hope of sway
O'er love's receding shore.

White the Light, His glorious might
Which scattered shades before
And bade us lay aside the fray
To fight His love no more.

Red flows down His tortured crown
And cleanses from within
Our wretched gown from brackish brown
To virgin wool again.

Purple His sash, covers our ash
And sackcloth loyalty,
Repents the lash, each painful gash
That bought our royalty.

These colors perceived, his gift received
Fills our hearts with joy
'Til love's conceived, and earth's believed
The song our hearts employ.

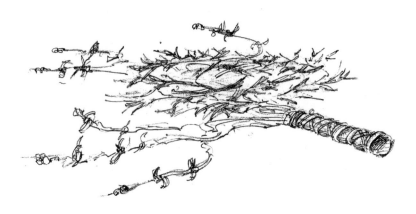

Lord, may my children find and keep that one true heart that sees through what they are to all they can become. Help them to love unconditionally in return. Amen.

FOR ADDITIONAL READING: ROMANS 5:8; JOHN 15:13; PROVERBS 10:12

FIFTY

Finishing

You've reached the end of a narrowing road,
A product of faithfully shouldering your load.
Now then give it all you've got,
Tell the world why you've struggled and fought
To hold your head above the rabble below
And hoe with assurance to the end of the row.

It's not in how much a man can begin,
But in what he can finish that the world measures him.

Lord of Rest, may my children find the joy of a job well done. May they discover that they cannot finish anything with their heads held high that they do not first commit to You and to your glory. Help them to go on when everyone is saying to quit. May they say with You, at the end of each daunting and impossible task completed, "It is finished!" Amen.

FOR ADDITIONAL READING: PHILIPPIANS 1:6; HEBREWS 12:2

FIFTY-ONE

Love Calling

The gift is all about the giver.

Fitful gusts blew random flakes into slowly deepening drifts under the dampened glow of hopeful street lamps that intermittently lit the path homeward with soft pools of light. Passed on the left and the right by package-laden shoppers too intent on wrapping deadlines to notice, the frail shivering frame of the elderly tottering man slowed to a halt. Glancing down at the yellowed face of his pocket watch, he carefully rubbed a weathered arthritic thumb across the fogged glass. "Still time," he mumbled to himself, resuming his trudge with renewed purpose.

By the time he had shuffled the two-and-a-half mile distance to the sidewalk that led to his humble dwelling, he was nearly exhausted, barely able to negotiate the last three steps up from the walk to the threshold of his tenement. The cold had stiffened his numb bare hands making it nearly impossible to grasp the right key and insert it into the lock. Finally, with a painful twist of the key and a shoulder pressed hard against the door, it yielded to admit the weary but grateful old man to his sparse yet homey abode.

Just then the heavy out-moded black phone on the end table next to his tattered easy chair came to life, breaking the stillness of the dimly-lit room. Smiling broadly to himself, he glanced at the family photo snapshot that leaned against the empty candy dish on the coffee table across the room and began to make his way to the phone. He answered on the third ring, "Hello? Grandson, is that you? ... And I love you and a merry Christmas to you, too!"

Heavenly Father, May my children always demonstrate the generosity of a grateful heart and so reveal your heart as the prime motivator in their giving. Amen.

FOR ADDITIONAL READING: LUKE 6:38; PROVERBS 11:24-25

FIFTY-TWO

Time and Speed

God's judgment is His mercy and time is a multiplier.
The earlier an error is detected and corrected, the less
the accumulated grief is borne.

The starlit scene was so serene
No hint of coming violence;
The countdown ticked and pale moon's rise
And anxious eyes searched empty skies,
The rocket poised in silence.

A sudden roar, convulsing shore
And flaming clouds of fire,
The gleaming ship rose in the night
On hopeful flight till out of sight,
A nation to inspire.

"All is well," the crew did tell,
"The flight path near perfection.
Trajectory close, though not quite true,
But it will do, for a day or two,
No time now for correction."

On they sped, as Earth's orb fled,
The rendezvous drew near.
But quick review of a wayward course
Revealed no force from any source
Could make the timely veer.

With growing fear that just a mere
Degree of error made,
Now multiplied by time and speed
And lack of heed to urgent need
Condemned their hopes to fade.

What might have been for these brave men
A glorious story told,
Instead a tragic tale became,
For timely aim removes the shame
Imprudence would unfold.

Patient Father, I thank you for the constant correction you have provided me, some of which I was not too distracted to heed. May Your Holy Spirit continue that work in my life and teach me how to perform for my children that same useful task. Amen.

FOR ADDITIONAL READING: HEBREWS 12:5-11; JOHN 14:15-17

Appendix

PROVERB:_____

_____

_____

_____

_____.

PARABLE (OR POEM):_____

_____

_____

_____

_____

_____

_____

_____

_____

_____

_____

_____

_____

_____.

PRAYER:_____

_____

_____

_____.

Alan E. Sargent

PROVERB:_____
_____
_____
_____
_____
_____.

PARABLE (OR POEM):_____
_____
_____
_____
_____
_____
_____
_____
_____
_____
_____
_____
_____
_____
_____
_____.

PRAYER:_____
_____
_____
_____
_____
_____.

PROVERB:_____

_____

_____

_____

_____

_____.

PARABLE (OR POEM):_____

_____

_____

_____

_____

_____

_____

_____

_____

_____

_____

_____

_____

_____.

PRAYER:_____

_____

_____

_____

_____

_____.

PROVERB:_____

_____

_____

_____

_____

_____.

PARABLE (OR POEM):_____

_____

_____

_____

_____

_____

_____

_____

_____

_____

_____

_____

_____

_____

_____.

PRAYER:_____

_____

_____

_____

_____

_____.

PROVERB:_____

_____

_____

_____

_____

_____.

PARABLE (OR POEM):_____

_____

_____

_____

_____

_____

_____

_____

_____

_____

_____

_____

_____

_____

_____.

PRAYER:_____

_____

_____

_____

_____

_____.

PROVERB:_____

_____

_____

_____

_____

_____.

PARABLE (OR POEM):_____

_____

_____

_____

_____

_____

_____

_____

_____

_____

_____

_____

_____

_____

_____.

PRAYER:_____

_____

_____

_____

_____.

PROVERB:_____

_____

_____

_____

_____

_____.

PARABLE (OR POEM):_____

_____

_____

_____

_____

_____

_____

_____

_____

_____

_____

_____

_____.

PRAYER:_____

_____

_____

_____

_____

_____.

PROVERB:_____
_____
_____
_____
_____
_____.

PARABLE (OR POEM):_____
_____
_____
_____
_____
_____
_____
_____
_____
_____
_____
_____
_____
_____.

PRAYER:_____
_____
_____
_____
_____.

Endnotes

1. Baron Lytton, *Richelieu*, Act II, Scene II (1839).

2. Rudyard Kipling, "If," in *Rewards and Fairies*, (New York: Doubleday, Page and Company, 1916) p. 181.

3. Oral Roberts, *The Miracles of Seed-Faith* (Tulsa: Oral Roberts Evangelistic Assn., 1970) pp. 66, 67.

4. *Declaration of Independence.*

5. David Crockett, *The Autobiography of David Crockett* (New York: Charles Scribner's Sons, 1923).

6. Copyright © Jay Erwin, Used by Permission; p. 155.

7. Thomas Henry Huxley, *"On Elemental Instruction in Physiology,"* in Huxley's Collected Essays, Vo. 3 (1877); pp. 299–300.